THIS DOES NOT LEAVE
THIS HOUSE

JULIE COONS

CONTENTS

"Your father never wanted you."

"I wish you had died at birth."

These words have so much power, especially when you're five. Especially when stated by your mother. Words can hurt deeply. She used them often, with emphasis, pretty much every time she was angry at me.

I prefer these words: I'm a survivor. I'm beautiful. I belong. I'm loved. I'm worth it. Most importantly, I have value and I am wanted.

This book is about my life. I am finally telling all the secrets I was never allowed to tell to encourage and motivate others to heal their own lives and break the cycle of abuse. I want to tell my story in the hope it will help others.

So often I felt so completely alone during the many struggles in my life. I was raised by an abusive, narcissistic mother. I was raped in college by a stranger. I married an abusive man that threatened to kill me if I ever tried to leave. His abuse nearly killed me anyway. My mother tried to trick me into having an abortion. I suffered physical and mental torment resulting in very low self-esteem. I tried to take my own life at some point along the way and a lot more that I haven't even mentioned yet. I want to help others and show that there is hope and life after abuse. My goal is that you can take my story and heal from it.

A couple of years ago, I went to see a spiritual medium. In the first second of sitting down with me, she knew I suffered from pancreatitis. She put her hand on her stomach, right exactly where my pain is located, looked at me, and said, "Unspeakable pain." Before this, I had always struggled with trying to describe my pain. With this, she validated to me she was the real deal since we had never met before.

Then the medium looked up to the corner of the room like she was listening to someone speak to her. "I have a message for you." *She told me later this was where her spirit guide was hovering.* Then she said, "The message I am supposed to give you is this: You need to write a book. It's an incredible story how you were able to escape from your abusive marriage and the cycles you were able to break." She added, "There are experiences in your life that need to be shared."

She then said, "Julie, it will really help others, too."

Those were the magic words I needed to hear. I have always felt that if something positive could come out of something so negative, then it was all worth it. I'm a major procrastinator and didn't start thinking about writing for another year. I went to visit Theresa again for some spiritual guidance, and then I got to work.

The first sentence was the hardest to write, just like the first step toward saving myself was the hardest to take. I was so scared to write this book because I used to hear "This does not leave this house" a lot growing up. Here I am divulging all the secrets. Even when Theresa was giving me a message from my father, who passed away in 2008, she had to first caution me that this message was not to be shared with anyone, or, in other words, "This does not leave this house." I figured that was just his way of validating to me it was truly him since I'd heard it so regularly from him growing up.

Why is it so important to break the cycle of abuse? Because breaking the cycle in your family will not only benefit your own children but their children too, and hopefully many generations to come. What could possibly be a better gift than to give your child a sense of safety and high self-esteem? It will also benefit generations of your family through time long after you are gone. Would that make you a hero? I believe it does.

I also fear I could anger a few people, but that's something I will deal with if it happens. I vow to be completely honest. If certain people don't like what I have to say, then they should reevaluate their own actions. I am also a little fearful of the feelings reliving the past could dredge up.

I have suffered from panic attacks since I was twenty-one. I remember exactly where I was and what I was doing when the first one hit. I thought I was going to die; it was horrible. I'm sure everyone else who has ever suffered with panic attacks can remember their first one as well. I certainly don't want to do anything that could bring those back up again. That said, it's still completely worth it. I have already spent too much time of my life in fear. Time to give this, as well as myself, a voice.

I strongly believe that forgiveness is something you give yourself, not the person whom you are forgiving. This is so important. It's hard on your soul to carry around so much dark energy that holding a grudge can create. It took me many years to totally understand this concept and put it to work. I'm better off for having done so. Still, there are those people I have struggled to forgive because I don't believe they deserve it. It's a process.

I'm also a big believer in karma. The times when I have wanted revenge the most are the times I had to just relax, put it in God's hands, and let the universe take care of it. It's amazing how often it did. Never as quickly as I would have liked, but I do believe karma did a much better job than I ever could have. Don't ever mess with karma.

This book is also about overcoming adversity and abuse and breaking cycles of abuse in families. I personally broke not just one but two cycles. I am so proud to say I was able to accomplish this, and, hopefully, generations long after mine will benefit. From what I have seen, not too many people are able to break these cycles. People live what they know. You might hate your parents because they were abusive and turn around and do the same exact things to your own children without even thinking about it. Hopefully, the lessons I learned will get passed on to others who read this, not just my family.

I'm not trying to sound all-knowing and all-powerful. That's just not who I am at all. Not even a little bit. It just happened for me, I think, because something must have triggered inside me that was so intense and powerful it automatically changed the cycle. I don't claim to have consciously set out to make an effort to change. For me, it was such an intense fear that, if I ever spanked my child, I wouldn't stop. I was terrified I would lose control. My parents constantly lost control, and many times they disciplined out of anger. From what I have experienced, disciplining out of anger is a dangerous thing. It also puts a lot of fear and trepidation into a child.

I felt so much love for my daughter when she was born. I wanted to shower her with affection every single day of her life because I too was in such need of it. I wanted to make sure she never doubted how much she was loved, and I also wanted her to have an incredible self-esteem. I never wanted her to fear me, not ever. I know for a fact that I accomplished this. The greatest compliment I have ever received was from my adult daughter when she thanked me for breaking the cycle. This to me is the greatest gift I could ever receive. Forever the best gift. My sweet girl is a very confident, self-assured adult, and I love watching her as a new mom. She has so much more confidence than I ever had, and it's truly a blessing.

I have heard people say things like, "How can you expect them to be good parents when they didn't have that themselves?" They say it like it's a legitimate excuse for abusing their children because they didn't know any better. What a crock. What I did was wrap up everything I wish I'd had in a mother and became that for my daughter. Instead of repeating the crappy cycle and putting it on my daughter because that was "all I knew," I thought about what kind of childhood I wish I'd had and tried my hardest to make it happen for her.

This book is about breaking cycles of abuse, conquering your fears, and getting out of abusive relationships. I experienced abuse as a child and then went on to marry an abusive man. This book aims to tell how I escaped abuse in my marriage and saved myself as well as my daughter.

It took almost an entire year to find just the exact right moment to leave my abusive husband. It's a very interesting story how I planned and executed my escape. I believed him when he said he would kill me if I ever left him. He was a hunter, and we had quite a few guns in the house, which I hated. He didn't want me, but he didn't want me to be free either. It's so hard to understand, let alone explain. I was so clever in my escape. Thankfully, I am still here and living proof that cycles of abuse can be broken.

However, before I go too deep into the marriage story, I will need to give a little prelude of my life so you can see why I even got involved with an abuser to begin with. I am taking you on a journey. A journey into darkness, then finally finding the light. Coming from where I was to being who I am today is something of a miracle. It will be painful at times, but if it helps anyone else, then it's worth it to me. It's amazing how fast things are flooding my mind. Amazing how much one person can experience in the span of a lifetime.

The journey starts now . . .

When I was two years old, I got deathly sick with an illness called nephritis. This affected my kidneys, similar to a serious infection but more dangerous because it could shut my kidneys down. My kidneys weren't working very well, and I blew up like a balloon because my body was retaining too much water. I was basically sent home to die. Doctors really didn't know how to treat this illness back in the sixties.

I eventually recovered, but ever since then I have battled frequent, intensely painful kidney infections. They used to call them kidney attacks. They made me very sick with really high fevers, and were extremely painful.

When I was fifteen, I got another one of my normal kidney infections, or so I thought. I was laying on the couch in a lot of pain and extremely nauseated. My mother was sitting in a chair next to the couch, talking on the phone incessantly, smoking one cigarette after another. The smell of the smoke intensified my nausea and caused me to throw up. Every time I asked her to stop smoking, she ignored me. I don't remember who she was talking to. It seemed like she was on the phone all day, smoking constantly.

As the day went on, I got increasingly ill, so I told her I needed some medical help. Again, she ignored me. My father managed a men's clothing store and worked a lot of hours. He finally came home that night after nine, just in time to see me pass out in the bathroom. My father called our neighborhood doctor for advice. Too bad the neighbor he called was an ophthalmologist. Luckily for me, the neighbor advised my father to call my medical doctor.

We met him at the local hospital. My parents pulled their car right up to the front door and a team of nurses ran out, put me on a gurney, and pushed me inside. I was too sick to be scared or anxious about what was happening. I was placed in a trauma room. I kept going in and out of consciousness.

All of a sudden, I felt myself floating in the corner of the room. It was like gently bouncing up and down in mid-air. I looked down at myself and saw that I was dressed in a hospital gown, and I could see everyone working on me below. *I could see me, my body lying there on the exam table.* I could easily see everything the nurses and my doctor were doing while they worked on me. They were all moving quickly and deliberately, as if something were really wrong. Even though that was my body on the table I was looking down at, it was as if I were watching someone else and I really had no concern about what was going on.

One of the nurses rolled me over and gave me a shot in the butt, then more people came into the room. I heard the word "sepsis" spoken, but I didn't have a clue at the time what it meant. I saw a big machine with paddles attached rushed into the room and thought I must be pretty sick. I knew what those paddles were for. I could also hear in the distance one of the nurses say, "Doctor, we're losing her." It was a very weird feeling and a scary thing to hear, but I didn't care. I was bathed in warmth and wasn't in any pain at all anymore. That was incredibly cool. I loved it.

I was more content than I had ever been in my entire life, plus I was out of pain for the first time in days. I can't even begin to explain how happy I felt to have the suffering completely gone. I wanted to stay where I was and out of pain forever. I felt peace and calm like I have never felt before. Then, all of a sudden, with no warning, I was blasted back into my body. I felt hands push me back—literally pushing me back into my body with incredible force. It was horrible. It was like hitting a brick wall at one hundred miles an hour. Intense pain hit me when I reentered my body. It was excruciating. "Can I please go back into the corner now?"

This sucks.

As soon as I could, I told my doctor and the other nurses in the room that I had been up in the corner watching them while they had worked on me. Nobody believed me. They said I was hallucinating. But when I began to share what I'd seen, recounting what each person was doing to me from the vantage point of the ceiling with precise accuracy, disbelief showed on their faces.

"How could you possibly know that?"

A nurse spoke what the others were surely thinking. "You were unconscious."

"No, I wasn't," I insisted. "I was hovering in the corner watching you."

A couple of the nurses seemed convinced. Out-of-body experiences hadn't become mainstream then. It felt as weird to me as it did to them. I didn't understand it myself, but I didn't mind it either. Anytime anything takes my pain away, I am grateful.

Whatever I had experienced, one thing is for sure. When I left my body, the illness that I had suffered did too. I must have come very close to the veil and was healed by the spirit world because I never had another kidney infection.

My experience wasn't like anything I had ever heard of. No bright light. Not even a vision of a spirit. I knew instinctively that I was in good hands. After I left the hospital, I never talked to anyone else about this. Who would believe me who hadn't been in that room?

No way could I tell my mother. She would just ridicule me.

☙ 3 ❧

I'm in a basement, I'm chained to my chair, and I'm six years old. First grade in my new Catholic school. I refer to my childhood as an experiment in terror. I had a crazy mom (*I lived with her, so I'm more than qualified to make this determination*) and I went to Catholic school in the '60s. If that wasn't bad enough, I'm left-handed, which was hugely looked down upon in the Catholic community. I never knew why; it just was. Maybe being different made you evil, I don't know. I believe anything that was outside of normal was looked upon as evil. All children are evil *in the nuns' opinion,* but the lefties are especially bad.

The nuns used to tie my left wrist to the side of my chair and put all my pencils and crayons in my right hand. I am extremely left-handed, so this was challenging to say the least. I just flat out couldn't use my right hand. So, next came the ruler punishment, public humiliation; any idea they could come up with to "inspire" me. I was only six years old and in new, unfamiliar territory. I didn't know it was wrong to be left-handed. So why are they treating me like I am some kind of freak? Why was being different so bad?

Maybe I am a freak.

There weren't any other kids in my class tied to their chair. Every time the teacher saw me try to wiggle out of the ties, I got hit across my fingers with the ruler. This stuff hurts.

"Lay your hand flat on the table and don't move," they would tell me.

Then rap, rap, rap came the ruler.

Ouch! That stings so bad! All this for being left-handed. Must be serious. The humiliation part came when the teacher mocked me to the whole class and wanted them to see me get hit with the ruler and cry. Kind of an example to the other little pests in the room to do as they are told. I am proud to say I am still a very strong lefty. *Screw them!*

Lunch time was also very enjoyable. They wouldn't let you bring your own lunch, so you had to eat what they served. I was a pretty picky eater back then. Basically, all I liked were hamburgers and french fries. I was so grateful for my big brother. He would crawl along under the tables in the school cafeteria, and, when he got to me, I would scrape my food onto his plate. The thing I remember them serving most was peanut butter and jelly sandwiches. Ick! And cooked spinach. Double ick! If we didn't eat everything on our plate, we would spend the entire recess with a nun staring down at us in the lunchroom. Luckily, my brother saved me that fate. It was both scary and intimidating.

Let me explain just how scary the nuns were. They wore these outfits they called "habits." They were all black with a headdress that looked like a scary hood. They were downright terrifying. I have heard them referred to as penguins in the past, but penguins are cute little animals, and these animals were anything but cute. Long black dresses with high necks and this thing that covered their heads and only showed a portion of their face. It was terrifying to look at them, especially as a little kid. I now refer to myself as a "recovering" Catholic. That was first grade, my introduction into torture.

I know of six people from Catholic school who have committed suicide. I will never forget a little boy named Randy in my class. He was always so nervous, and because of that he pooped his pants on a regular basis. It usually fell out his pant leg. This was somehow a gift to our nun, Sister Mary Goretti. I called her Sister Mary Gorilla. She would publicly mock this poor child and encouraged the other kids to mock him and laugh at him as well. It broke my heart and brought me to tears to see him being treated this way.

He just stood there. It was heart-wrenching. I prayed for it to end. I am surprised I didn't get paddled for crying and not joining in on mocking him like the rest of the class. You know those moments in life that don't seem real even though it's happening right in front of your face? This was one of those moments. Unfortunately, this wasn't a one-time occurrence. It happened many times. Poor kid was too afraid of the teacher to ask to leave to go to the bathroom. Years later, he took his own life.

Another kid walked in front of a train. One put some plastic down on the floor in a room at Motel 6 and shot himself in the head. Two others overdosed, and I think another one drank some Drano. What a terrible way to go. I remember thinking how thoughtful the boy that shot himself at the Motel 6 was to put the plastic down. He didn't want to make a mess for others, but also how very calculated and planned out this suicide was. I also wondered why all the suicides were boys. Years later, when the sexual allegations came out against the church, I stopped wondering.

I still can't wrap my head around why the nuns thought it was OK to mistreat us. What was in it for them? What was their reward? Were they just so sadistic they enjoyed it? In my opinion, they were just plain evil. But wait, this was a religious school. Hard to imagine the things that went on under the noses of willing parents that paid for their kids to go to these schools, let alone accepting the fact that it was *all* real.

I threw up almost every day before school. I begged my parents not to take me there. They had paid a lot of money for us to be treated this way. I didn't understand it. It seemed like a group of frustrated women who wanted to torture small children got together and became nuns. This was probably written in the job description back in the '60s. You want to torture small children and get paid for it? Become a nun, spelled n-o-n-e. I will admit it: I strongly hated these women. I'm sure I still do. It's sad to say I don't think this pain will ever leave me. I couldn't imagine ever sending my daughter to a school like this. There are stains on our society, and this is definitely one of them.

I was the hero in my school in the second grade. I had a Chipmunks record I liked and wanted to share it with the class. I got approval from Sister Gorilla, *much to my surprise,* to bring it to school one day. Well, as everyone knows, the Chipmunks normally sound like the record was turned up to a higher speed, but that's just their regular voices. However, somehow my teacher wasn't aware of that. She accused me of turning up the speed, and when I tried to explain to her I hadn't, she sent me to Mother Superior's office for talking back. *This was where corporal punishment took place.*

You know that paddle game with the ball on the string that always broke off and then all you had left was just a paddle? Well, if you ever won one of those at a school carnival, you lost it as fast as you could. All of mine ended up in the trash, which is probably the first place the nuns looked for them. They drilled holes in the paddles and used them on our little fannies. Her instructions were to bend over, grab your ankles, and wait for the beating. I could hear the wind going through the paddle. I ducked, she lost control of the paddle, and it hit the wall and broke in half. This made her even angrier, so she suspended me from school for two weeks. *There really IS a God!* Two weeks away from this place? That's a vacation. She called my mother, yelled at her for a while for not controlling her kid, then told her to come get me. I wonder how many of those calls mom got between my brother and me. I'm sure it was a lot.

Did you know that throwing up in church could get you suspended from school? I didn't know this either at the time it happened to me. I was in second grade. The nuns had arranged what would be considered an unusual field trip by any measure. They were taking us to a funeral at the church.

We didn't need a bus. The church stood across the parking lot from the grade school. The whole student body, grades 1-6, were marched across the parking lot and paraded into the church. It was an open casket funeral. I can still remember the man's face. I had never seen a dead body before. It freaked me out so much, I couldn't do it. I couldn't sit there and stare at a dead body. I was feeling weak and panicky. I started imagining that was me inside that casket. I started fidgeting and grew more nauseous as time went on. Unfortunately for me, I was sitting next to Sister Mary Goretti. I mean, Sister Gorilla.

I kept telling her I needed to leave because I was going to be sick. She wouldn't let me leave and told me sternly to sit there, behave, and be quiet. Well, I had to throw up, so I leaned over and threw up on her foot. That finally got me a trip out of there and onto a chair against the wall in the cafeteria which was inside a door next to the church. She told me to sit there and not move, which is exactly what I did. At least now I'm away from that dead body and can finally try to recover from the trauma.

After the funeral, the entire school was paraded back to the school in front of me. Humiliation was the word of the day because I had thrown up on the chair next to me a couple more times. The nuns allowed the entire school to walk past me and laugh at me on their way out. I just sat there and cried. It was so horrible. Then, again, back to Mother Superior's office, another paddling, and a call to my mother to come get me. I got suspended for two weeks, which was my reward for the torture I had just endured.

In a surprisingly rare turn of events, my mother turned her wrath on the nuns. She yelled at them for taking her kid to an open casket funeral without her permission, then she took me out for a milkshake. It was the most loving thing I think Mom has ever done for me. She also tried to get my father to let us kids out of Catholic school, but he wouldn't hear of it. My father was the epitome of a died-in-the-wool Catholic. He went to Catholic school and, by golly, his kids would go there, too. *Don't think of breaking any cycles here, Dad.* I guess if it was good enough for him, it was good enough for us.

Another time I got sick was in the nuns' convent, which was next door to the school. I threw up in their kitchen sink. The nuns' house, where they all lived together, is called a convent. There was only one nun with me. No other children or nuns were present. I wonder now why I was singled out and why I was the only child in their living quarters. I don't remember much, but I do remember the nun was extremely angry that I threw up in their sink. She was a lot angrier than you would expect someone to get. She called my mother and yelled at her again for not controlling her child better and asked her to come pick me up. Mom came to the convent to get me, and I think she even wondered why I was in their private living quarters. Regardless, I probably dodged a bullet that day. It was like being broken out of prison every time I escaped that wretched place.

I had finally completed my prison sentence and was set free from this horrible school at the end of sixth grade. I was allowed to go to public school and I loved it. Nobody there ever hit me or ridiculed me or humiliated me. It was wonderful. I flourished, too. The other kids there seemed happier, too, and they all wanted to get to know me. It was here I learned that I had a real knack for making people laugh. I felt I could be myself for the first time in my life. I could relax and stop looking over my shoulder and stop feeling afraid that I was going to be abused for anything I said or did. For the first time in my life, I didn't wake up feeling nauseous at the thought of going to school. I thought I was finally free.

I quickly realized that I was advanced compared to my new classmates, but what sacrifices had I made to get there? I don't even want to think about it. The nuns broke a lot of rulers, but they didn't break me. Not completely anyway.

There is so much of my childhood I have blocked out and forgotten. I have considered trying hypnotism to help me remember but then decided against it. Maybe what is forgotten needs to stay forgotten. I think there is a very good reason I am not remembering some things. I think our brains are our best and most powerful tool to protect us against horrible memories.

I tried hypnotism once to quit smoking, but it never worked. I purchased ten sessions at a place in Portland for close to two thousand dollars. The drive there was an hour each way, and I smoked all the way home after supposedly being hypnotized to quit. Each time, they told me I was really hypnotized, but I knew I wasn't. I kept trying to tell them that I knew everything they said to me and I was present the entire time. Their disbelief was so frustrating. Were they afraid I would ask for my money back? Is it possible that some people just cannot be hypnotized?

One person was quite adamant to the point of getting angry with me, insisting that I had been cured. I gave up, walked out of the office, got in my car, and lit up a cigarette. I think it was a scam, but maybe it's because I was too afraid to let my guard down. I was too scared to let a stranger operate my brain. I have had too many years being on high alert. Anytime I relaxed and let my guard down, bad things happened.

I'm guessing that my brother didn't fare too well in Catholic school either. We never talked about it, and now we just plain never talk. He's an angry guy. I've heard he's been court-ordered to attend three separate anger management courses. I don't know why my brother is so angry. Is it from years of abuse by the Catholic school or was it from our screwed-up home life?

He's not very nice to me and acts like he's hated me most of my life. I was told that my brother wouldn't even look at me after I was born. It took him two weeks after I came home from the hospital to look at me. A few days later, Mom found him holding me upside down by my ankles over the toilet. *That would have been a horrible demise.* He was three when I invaded his world and I'm not sure he ever got over it.

There was a short period of time during college we got along, and I'm forever grateful for those memories. He lived at the SAE fraternity. Many Sunday nights, we went out to dinner together because the cook at the frat house didn't work on Sunday. We usually had "garbage grinder" burgers at O'Callahan's. I felt like we grew closer during those times. I always wanted my big brother to like me. I was the little sister who always wanted attention from her big brother. When I visited him in college, I would get up early, go to the grocery store so I could secretly fill his kitchen up with food, and usually left him money on the counter. Now I look back and wonder if I was trying to buy his affection.

I have many memories worrying my head off over my brother. He liked to party a lot in high school, and I knew he had cologne in his glove box to hide the alcohol on his breath. I'm not sure Mom and Dad were aware of what he was doing, but I was, and it caused me many sleepless nights. I used to stand at my window in my bedroom watching for him, and when I got extra worried I would start to pray. He usually pulled in around three in the morning. He never knew I did that, and I think it would come as quite a surprise to him. I think it was easier for him to convince himself that I didn't care about him either.

One time at a party, I talked with an old girlfriend of his from high school. She shared that he always seemed to be afraid of our parents. I was really shocked to hear her say that. I always thought it was just me. The truth is, I admired and loved him a lot and wanted to be just like him. I'm sorry we don't speak anymore. We are the only two people on the planet who know what it was really like to grow up in a home like ours. We could probably really support each other, but I doubt if that will ever happen.

I used to crawl under my bed when I heard him getting hit from our father down the hall in his room when we were kids. I used to lay under my bed and cry and pray for his beatings to end. Dad even used to brag to others about how his watch would cut into his wrist from beating my brother. A few times he even used his belt on him. I would pray to the point of near hysteria, and that's when it would stop. I never heard a single cry from my brother during those beatings. He was too stubborn or too proud, I guess.

I was desperate for love and attention no matter where it came from. Mom and Dad wanted to turn their backs on him many times, usually when he asked them for money, but they ended up helping him after I talked them into it.

Ironically, in the end, he turned his back on me.

4

The basic stuff you get from a parent is just touch and affection and feeling valued. I don't remember my mother telling me she loves me, not even once. I am so proud I broke this horrible cycle. Not a single day goes by that I haven't told my daughter I love her at least one time. Unlike my brother, my abuse was more mental than physical. Most of it came from my mother. She liked to tell me that my father never wanted me and that she wished I had died at birth. What kind of mother tells her daughter she wished she had died at birth? This wasn't a one-time occurrence. It happened frequently. Be careful what you say, especially when you are angry. Some things are impossible to take back.

In my mother's case, she never tried to take it back, nor did she ever apologize for any of it. Most of the time she denied she even said it. She was famous for saying, "I did not," or, my all-time favorite, "You're lying," and, of course, "That never happened."

I'm not sure which was worse in my childhood: the Catholic school experience during the day or going home to my crazy mother after school. The first evidence I saw that she wasn't normal was when I was four. We had just finished eating dinner. Mom and Dad were busy cleaning the kitchen when the phone rang. Shortly after Mom answered it, she completely freaked out. She slammed the phone down, grabbed a knife, and ran out of the house.

My father told my brother to watch me, then he ran after her. She ran out of the house, screaming, "He's coming to kill me!" OK, so I am four years old and about to lose my mother. Now I am freaked out too. Nobody could console me, especially not my seven-year-old brother, if he even cared to try. I was shaking and crying and in a state of complete panic. She wasn't gone long, and I was very happy to see her walk back through the door. That was when the craziness started, and it lasted for decades. I don't have a relationship at all with my mother today. The last thing she said to me was that she wouldn't care if I died. She is just too toxic for my peace of mind.

Mom seemed to enjoy imposing mental torment more than physical abuse. I got very good at being able to tell when things were turning wonky. Her eyes got a little glazed over and even a slight bit darker. She would whisper most of the crazy stuff in my ear, which took her threats to a whole new level of intensity with pure crazy creepiness.

"You are going to find me dead when you come home from school today," she whispered. On a different day, she would speak of a different way she would die. Hanging herself in different parts of the house. Taking some pills. Cutting her wrists. Why did she have to whisper this to me all the time? Who says this stuff to a little kid? I was a cute, petite, sickly little child who always feared she was going to lose her mom.

I begged my father to get her some help and make her stop. When I was in grade school, this stuff really scared me. I needed a mother and couldn't understand why mine always wanted to leave us. All the other kids probably had mothers who were loving and kind. Why can't I have a mother like that? She got the biggest reaction from me, which is probably why the torment continued with just me for the rest of my childhood. I used to plead, cry, and beg her not to leave me. I would be terrified all day in school wondering if this was going to be the day I lost my mother. These fears she constantly put in my head made it even harder for me to concentrate while tied to my chair.

I never once told anyone about this either. First of all, I was terrified of the nuns and avoided them as much as possible. How was I to know telling something like this wasn't going to get me into trouble? I mean, I am already tied to my chair for being left-handed. What could this information do to me? I would never confide anything to any nun. They terrified and intimidated me. I can't even relate to people when they tell me they loved their grade-school teachers. I looked upon all of mine, not as a friend who wanted to help me, but as my enemy. Who wouldn't though, if you were constantly being beaten down by them both physically and mentally? Weird thing is, I had a terrible mother. Why did I care if she left me or not?

By the time I got to middle school, this had just become my normal. Today, I believe I would have been better off if she had killed herself. She was a horrible mother. She was also the first person to tell everyone what a great mother she was. My father never once encouraged or forced her into getting any help. I am pretty sure he was more afraid of her than he would ever admit. This is the reason why he allowed us kids to endure her sick punishments instead of stepping in to help us. Heaven forbid she would turn on him if he tried. My brother and I constantly begged him for help. He worked from nine in the morning until nine or later in the evening, six days a week. My father abandoned his kids and allowed us to take the wrath of our mother instead of stepping up to help us. I guess he would rather have been at work than at home dealing with his crazy-ass wife.

The last time she threatened me where I actually gave a crap was when I was seventeen. I was getting ready for school and again she whispered in my ear how I was going to find her dead when I got home. Why did she pick this day? She knew what a big day it was for me.

I was a high school varsity cheerleader. I loved being a cheerleader. It took me three years of trying out to make the squad, and I wanted to enjoy every single minute of it. I loved wearing my cheerleader uniform to school. I didn't even care when my World Lit teacher took every opportunity he could to tell me how worthless he thought cheerleaders were, of course, in front of the entire class. He even announced that he was on the school board and had petitioned against allowing cheerleaders at the school. Every time I walked into his classroom while wearing my uniform set him off on his little rants. *Don't be a hater, Mr. Whiteman.* I was proud of my little accomplishment and nobody was taking this away from me.

Well, almost nobody . . .

I decided I had to go to school. I couldn't stay home and babysit my mom. I couldn't stop thinking about her threat, so when it was time for my lunch break I went to the pay phone and called her to make sure she was OK. She didn't answer the phone. I panicked. Had she actually gone through with one of the threats she had made over the years?

Today was a very important day for me and for our high school. Our basketball team was going to state championships that weekend. This pep assembly was a big deal and I had to be there. I was torn for a moment. The other cheerleaders and I had practiced for weeks to perform a dance routine for the entire school, and the other girls were counting on me to be there. But this is my mother, and she could be lying dead or dying at home.

With surprising ease, I made the choice to abandon my team. I ran all the way home to check on my mother. I knew I would definitely miss the pep assembly. When I got home, she wasn't anywhere in sight. Panicking, I went back outside to look for her. I saw a neighbor and asked her if she had seen my mom. She told me she was heading downtown to do some shopping.

Shopping? You bitch! Why are you constantly trying to ruin my life? Now I have to go back to school and face the other girls whom I had abandoned. What could I possibly say to them? Remember, "This does not leave this house," *my father always said with teeth clenched.* I wasn't allowed to tell anyone what went on in my house, nor could I deal with the shame of my friends knowing the truth. I racked my brain as I walked back to school, hot tears streaming down my face. What would I tell them? I couldn't concentrate. This was the most important day in my life as a cheerleader. It was my last pep assembly ever, the most important day of my life up to this point, and I am missing it. Too much turmoil, too much drama. I was beyond stressed out walking all the way back to school. I would just have to lie, say I got sick or something, but never tell what was really going on. Never,

ever could I let out the truth. What was true from that day on is I never gave another thought to my mother's stupid threats.

When I was twenty-one, I worked as a teller at a bank downtown. Mom's birthday came around, and I invited some family members over to my parents' house to celebrate. I had invited my Aunt Jeannine over to eat dinner with the three of us before her party. I was still trying to please my mother. I was going to attempt to cook her a nice birthday dinner of fried chicken, mashed potatoes, and green beans. So, after work I ran to the store, bought everything for dinner, and hurried over to their house. Aunt Jeannine is my mom's sister and I absolutely adored her. She was normal compared to my mother, and she always showed love and kindness to me. I also look like I could be one of her kids. She has four kids, so she used to tell me that I was actually one of her kids but she couldn't raise us all and gave me to her sister. She was kidding, of course, but how desperately I wished she weren't.

In the middle of cooking dinner, Mom disappears. Dad went looking for her, and we learned that she had taken a bottle of wine out of the kitchen, went upstairs, and locked herself in her bedroom. When Dad told me she had locked herself in her bedroom, I went looking for her favorite Carlo Rossi Vin Rose wine and discovered it was missing too. She was famous for locking herself in her room but never without her bottle of wine. When Dad tried to get her to come down the stairs to be with us, she refused. She wouldn't even give him a reason for this new drama of hers. By the time Aunt Jeannine arrived, Mom had been locked in her room for over an hour. It was time for dinner, so Dad tried one last time to get her to come downstairs to eat dinner with us. Again, she refused. *Really, Mom? Are you kidding me with this? What is your problem now? I bust my ass to make you a nice birthday dinner and you can't get yours out of your bedroom?*

Aunt Jeannine, Dad, and I had a nice dinner together without discussing a strategy for dealing with the arriving birthday guests. What would we say to explain why the birthday girl wasn't there? How embarrassing. Aunt Jeannine went upstairs and told Mom she was disgusted by what she was doing to her daughter. Mom threatened to jump out of the window of her bedroom in response. I had gotten up the stairs in time to hear her new threat.

I was so furious! "Go ahead, Mom!" I yelled at her through the door. "See if I care!" I was so angry and just plain fed up. I had worked really hard to make it a nice birthday for her and this is how she shows appreciation? She was being so rude. Long overdue anger took over me, and dear Aunt Jeannine saw it. She was also fed up and decided to get me out of there. We actually left my father there alone to deal with the two guests who had showed up, along with my mother locked away. *Time for you to deal with her now, Dad. I'm out of here.*

She drove me downtown to the nearest bar. She called her two daughters to come join us and we all got drunk. I never thought anybody knew how crazy my mother was or knew any of the crap she was putting her family through. I always felt so alone with zero support and nobody to talk to. It was quite surprising to me when Aunt Jean told me that everyone in the family knew my mother was nuts. My big secret was out. *What a relief.* Now I can get some things off my chest. Thank you, Aunt Jean!

My mother was all about outward appearances and fooling the world. Her favorite saying was "dripping in diamonds." My father worked very hard to make sure she was. I have many stressful memories of Christmas shopping for her with my father. He would ask the sales clerks to try clothes on to make sure they were good enough for her. Dad was always a nervous wreck, beginning with shopping and accelerating on Christmas morning, when our efforts would be intensely judged. She had to have a little blue box every year from "Jackson's," the local high-end jewelry store. Her favorite dress store was "LaPointe's," so very important there were gift boxes with the name "LaPointe's" on them as well. Hell to pay if she wasn't pleased. She could ruin Christmas for everyone.

We would have to apologize for letting her down and reassure her that we really didn't hate her. Somehow, it meant we didn't love her if we didn't spend enough money on her. If she didn't like her presents, it meant we didn't like her. I really hated Christmas. Her rants were intense and could go on for days. She would scream at me for hours and sometimes it even got physical: ripping earrings out of my ears and scratching the backs of my hands until they bled. She was mentally ill, but I didn't know it until later. As an adult, I was finally successful at getting her to a professional who could diagnose her disorder and get her the medication she needed. Getting her to stay on it, however, was an even bigger challenge.

I have often wondered if my father had some Mafia ties. He spent a lot of money on fashion, jewelry, cars, private schools, etc. on a men's clothing store manager's budget. The Mafia was very involved in men's clothing back in the sixties. Dad used to go to buying shows, and he usually came home with stories to tell about what happens when someone crosses the Mafia. There was this one buying trip where a man was found murdered in a hotel room down the hall from my father's. He was found with a certain appendage cut off and stuck in his mouth. My father said that was a calling card of the Mafia. I learned at a very early age you should never cross the Mafia. I have no proof he was involved, but I always wondered how he afforded our lifestyle.

Today, I am fairly convinced my mother had a shopping addiction. She took me shopping all the time with her. When I was too young for school, she would drop my brother off, then she would head downtown dragging me from store to store, most of the time forgetting to feed me. Mom would get very angry when clothes shopping for me because, in her opinion, nothing ever fit me. She often said, "Too bad you have the family butt," referring to my father's side of the family. Was she trying to say everyone in his family had a big butt? She certainly wanted me to think I did, that's for sure. My brother used to call me a freak of nature. He regularly told me, "If you want to be top-heavy, walk on your hands," referring to my butt.

My mother never lacked for self-esteem, probably because she stole all of mine. She used to laugh when my brother mocked me. She had to dress in the finest clothes, wear the finest jewelry, and get her hair done every week. Outward appearances are what mattered to her. And that applied to her children, too. She used to mock me a lot for being fat, but when I look back on photos taken of me when I was young, I was never fat. One day, while looking at some family photos with my husband, he commented, "You're not fat in any of these pictures."

I was constantly on a diet, not by my own doing but my mother's. I'm very happy in life now, but I look back and I feel so sorry for the little girl I used to be. My mother told me that when I was two, the owner of Meier & Frank (now Macy's) asked her if she would let me model in a fashion show they were having. My mother said no because she didn't want me to get a big head or act stuck up. Well, it appears she accomplished that goal and then some. I am the furthest thing from stuck up, but I really could have used a little positive reinforcement. Didn't she say I was only two? Come on! I believe she just didn't want any attention to be on me. Heaven forbid I should take any attention away from her. *What could possibly be worse than a stuck up two-year-old?*

I always felt uncomfortable when it was my birthday and people came to our house with presents for me. My self-worth was so low I used to feel bad they had to come over and bring me a present. These people were all there for me, and it didn't make me feel good. It made me feel embarrassed and apologetic. I hated being the center of attention. Because of my experience, I came to understand that self-worth is a very important gift to give to a child. The real reason I was so embarrassed is that I didn't believe I was worth it.

This was my "normal." I didn't know what a normal mother was, and I certainly didn't know that other children had better lives than mine. I remember going over to a friend's house down the street and her mother treated her like she was a princess. She was so kind and loving and actually told her daughter she loved her right in front of me. She made us Spaghetti-o's for lunch and built us a little picnic in their backyard. I remember thinking her mother must either be fake, crazy, or really love her. So many times, I wished I could go live with my friends. They all seemed to have such loving mothers.

Like most adolescents and teens, my friends were important to me. My friends were my love supply. Well, friends and chocolate. I never brought any of them to my house, except for my closest friend, Kathy. I confided in her a lot and trusted her completely. She was my very best friend in high school. She was the only person I allowed over to see the embarrassment that was my mother, but nobody else was invited. I couldn't risk letting my mother get too close because she enjoyed bad-mouthing her children too much. She would do anything in her power to cause me to lose my friends. Nobody likes shit talked about them behind their back, but, when it comes from your own mother, it cuts deep. Anything negative she learned about me could and would be used against me. I can't count how many friends I have lost because of things she said about me, real or imagined. What kind of mother bad-mouths their own children? *Is this normal?* Well, it was my normal, unfortunately.

I will always be grateful for my grandma, Eva, my father's mom. She was the one woman in my life who showed me what unconditional love felt like. I have so many amazing, fun memories of my grandma even though she died when I was only six. The earliest memory I have of Grandma Eva was when I was still in diapers, lying on her chest, sleeping with my butt up in the air. It's strange, but I actually remember this. Grandma was stout and so very comfy. Grandma was always happy and singing and just joyful to be around. There was never a stressful moment when I was with her. She was like a breath of fresh air.

Grandma made all my Barbie clothes for me. They were so beautiful. My Barbie had a fancy wedding dress she made too. She also made me quilts that I am so blessed to still have. She made me an apron with a horse appliqué on the front and my name above it. I also had an Easy-Bake Oven at her house. In one of my favorite pictures, I am standing on a chair in her kitchen with my go-go boots and my little apron on over my dress, and I am making my brother cakes with my Easy-Bake Oven.

Grandma taught me how to crochet when I was only three. She was amazingly talented and I loved to sit on her lap and watch her crochet. Since I was left-handed and she was right-handed, it was the perfect way to teach a lefty how to crochet since it was backward for me. It was the easiest thing I can ever remember learning. It came so naturally for me, and it was something I really enjoyed doing with my grandma. One day, I just picked it up and started crocheting.

She also had a piano that I loved to pound on while she made up songs to go with it. Because of her influence, I went on to take nine years of piano lessons and became quite an accomplished pianist. Grandma and I did everything together and walked everywhere since she didn't drive a car. We walked to church early in the morning and then to the "Duck Inn," where we got chocolate-dipped ice cream cones and fed the ducks. Grandma was very involved in her church and walked to early mass every day. She always dressed up and wore high heels. She loved to play cards with her friends and drink wine in the afternoon. She even cussed when the card games didn't go her way! She was a wonderful cook and was in the process of fixing us dinner the day she died.

What an awesome tribute that my daughter named her daughter Eva. I cried the day she told me the name they picked. Stephanie told me it was because I always spoke about how giving and loving Grandma was and how much she helped others, as well as the fact I never said one negative thing about her. She was a really good, generous, and kind woman, and Stephanie wants her daughter to be just like her. Talk about coming full circle. What an honor, and my Grandma Eva deserves every bit of it. If I am half as good a grandma as my Grandma Eva was, I will be pretty incredible.

It's so strange. I have always felt her close to me, even after she died. I wasn't allowed to go to her funeral. I was too young in my parents' opinion. My brother and I were watched by our neighbors, the Curtises, the day of the funeral. I was so out of sorts that day. I remember that they took us out for hamburgers and milkshakes in their brand new Mustang. I was sitting in the front seat on Mrs. Curtis's lap and dropped my milkshake all over the floor of their new car. I cried and cried. I felt so bad for ruining their car. They were such nice people that they didn't seem to mind at all. Marge gave me the sweetest hug, and I secretly wished that she was my mother, too.

Grandma's funeral was at St. Joseph Catholic Church, where she had always attended, and it was standing room only the day of her funeral. I was told that the church was filled with people and there was a line out the door. It seemed like the whole town had come out to pay tribute to my grandma. She was a saint among women, and especially kind to me. I wish I could have been there. If she treated everyone the way she treated me, then no wonder the church was packed. My grandma died fifty years ago and I still miss her. I used to feel so robbed losing her, but I know she is still with me.

五

I always dreamed of becoming a pediatrician. I had been a very sick child, and I wanted to help other children someday. I have dealt with painful illnesses my entire life, starting when I was two and diagnosed with nephritis, a very serious kidney illness. I endured so many kidney tests that I developed an allergy to the dye. This required a needle in the arm, putting in special dye, and then the X-ray.

Usually, there were other kids in the room crying because they had to drink the "chalky" drink for their upper GI test. I knew the X-ray techs pretty well, so they always said, "Julie, get them to drink the stuff," and then they left the room. I never failed getting them to drink it either. I would see a child crying, and, when the tech left, I would call out to them.

"Hey, come over here a second," I would say. "See the needle in my arm? They said you could either drink the chalky drink or they could give it to you this way." Every time I did this, they drank it so incredibly fast. Now that I think back, I should have charged those techs a fee for my help.

I think I am a bit of a miracle myself. Because of the kidney problems I was having, I was told that my kidneys were getting weaker and I would eventually need dialysis and quite possibly a kidney transplant. I was also told I would never be able to have children because my kidneys couldn't handle the extra burden. This made me especially sad. I was born to be a mom. Thank goodness I had the out-of-body experience and was allowed to be healed. I was blessed with a miracle in the form of a daughter and now an incredibly cool granddaughter.

With the early understanding that I would need a lot of money for medical school, I started babysitting at the age of eleven. My first job was to watch a baby next door who was only two weeks old. I was very uneducated in the ways of babies, such as where they came from, etc. The lady next door was very open and almost hippic-like. She asked me if I wanted to see how a baby ate, which I thought was weird because I have seen babies drink out of a bottle many times.

So, not to be rude, I agreed. "Yes, of course." I wasn't prepared at all when she pulled out a breast and began to feed her baby. My reaction was to quickly exit their house and run back home. The neighbor called and told my mother what had happened, and Mom sent me right back over there. I was so embarrassed, but the neighbor understood and was very kind about it. I didn't want to ever face her again, but I'm glad I went back. I ended up being their babysitter for many years and worked for other families in the neighborhood. I became the number one person to call for babysitting on our street. I was a hard worker and very proud to be in high demand.

I saved every penny for college because I knew my father was going to help my brother and not me. He felt it was more important for his son to go to college because his daughter could "just get married," as he told me. I wasn't raised to feel very strong as a woman. I lived in a very male-centric family where women are beneath the men and very disposable. The men ruled. The women were weak and needed to be taken care of. I am glad that I came to know that this mindset is complete bullshit. What you are about to read is a story of strength, sheer tenacity, and an example of how amazing the human will is to survive, including a close brush with death that I am still here to talk about. After this all happened and I came out the survivor, I realized: I am powerful, not despite, but because of, my gender.

I took every college credit class I could in high school and then applied to the University of Oregon pre-med program. I worked very hard at everything I did, from babysitting to working in canneries in the summer and at a hair salon on the weekends. I enjoyed working in the cannery, and I especially loved working in the hair salon. I have always taken pride in whatever job I did. As long as I did it to my best ability, I could allow myself to feel proud. Two of the girls who worked in the hair salon and the one gay guy would work together to put my long hair up really fancy for our school dances. Back in the late '70s, it was almost a requirement to put your hair up with a ton of babies' breath sprinkled in. I looked like an English garden when they were done with me. I never felt more beautiful.

The day came when I learned that I had been accepted for the pre-med program at the University of Oregon. I was ecstatic I had been chosen. Finally, my dream was starting to come true. *This is the best thing that has ever happened in my life.* I could escape the craziness of my home life and really make something great out of myself. I couldn't get there fast enough.

College is a far cry from high school, that's for sure. Signing up for classes was very confusing for me. I accidentally signed up for a third-year genetics class. The teacher was a doctor from a foreign country who had written his own textbook. There were three hundred kids in his class, and I could barely understand a word he said.

After about a month, I went to his office one day for help because I was really struggling. It was so strange because all this stuff had come so easily for me in high school. I felt like I was an alien from another planet in college. When I met my teacher, the first thing he asked me was my age. "Young lady, you are in the wrong class," he stated after I told him. "This is a third-year genetics class and you will definitely fail."

It was too late to get my money back, and what did he just say? Did he say I would fail? Well, I guess I will just have to prove him wrong, won't I? I studied so hard, missed a ton of frat parties, and closed myself off in a dismal study room at the end of my dorm hallway. I managed to get a B in that class. I was so proud. *I am going to be an amazing physician someday and save a lot of lives*, I thought. Things were finally looking up in my life. I knew where I was going and nothing was going to stop me.

Well, almost nothing . . .

I went through rush to choose a sorority, but, unfortunately, I never got invited to the sorority I wanted. I remember the morning I got the tragic news. I was so upset. I went over to my brother's fraternity, crying my eyes out in the rain, and knocked on his bedroom window. He woke up, hungover from the party the night before, walked out of his room, closing the door behind him, and accidentally locked himself out. I was so upset and needed to talk to my brother, but he was too angry to listen because he was locked out of his room in the rain at seven in the morning. What a mess. Not a lot of support here, but what was I expecting? My bad for expecting my brother to be supportive.

I wanted to be a DG girl, Delta Gamma. The cutest and most popular girls on campus were in this sorority. So, because I hadn't already secured a dorm room, they were already taken, and all that was left with any availability was the University Inn. I had to take whatever roommate was given to me as well. The good thing about the University Inn was that the front doors were always locked. The price for that security was steep. It was nearly three times more expensive than the dorms.

The food there was amazing. Thirty football players were housed there on the second floor. I met a football player named Paul Renstrom. He was a really big guy and I realized why after eating with him a few times. I have never seen anybody eat as much as he did. He always called me "Mom." Finally, I asked him why he called me that all the time, and he said it was because I was made to be a mom. I always said, "No, Paul, I am going to be a doctor." We got to be very close friends, and he was a good friend to me at a time when I really needed one.

I had a roommate assigned to me named Veronica. We didn't know each other. I was desperate and had to take what they gave me. She was nice and shorter than me, which is rare. I am a whopping five-foot-one-and-a-half-inches tall. Finding someone shorter is not that easy. She was a cute, little Asian girl but not too much into being friends with girls. She preferred the boys. I didn't get to know her very well, and I really don't remember too much about her.

One night, she had a male guest in our room *as usual* and asked me to leave so they could be alone for a while. It seemed like she had a different guy in the room every night. I didn't want to make her angry, so I obliged and went down to the TV room on the second floor. There was another person there watching TV, a guy I had never seen before. We chatted for a while, and he seemed like a nice person. I noticed it was getting late and I was getting a stomachache. So, at three in the morning, I decided to go back to my room. I announced to this guy that I was going back to my room because I needed something for my stomachache.

He said, "Please don't go. I am really enjoying talking to you, plus I'm sure I have something in my room that will help you."

So, being the polite person that I am, as well as too trusting, *naïve really,* and not wanting to hurt any feelings, I said OK. He said his room was conveniently next to the TV room, so I said, "OK, I will stay a little longer and chat with you. Thanks."

His room was visible from the TV room, which I thought was a little strange. Most of the dorm rooms were behind a door and down a long hallway apart from the TV room. Right as he opened the door to his room, I knew I was in trouble. This wasn't a real dorm room at all, but a small, empty room, a little larger than a supply closet. On the counter sat a large butcher knife, which he immediately picked up and put against my throat while instructing me not to make a single sound.

Wait! What's happening?

He didn't really live here. Somehow, he'd snuck in and waited for a trusting victim like myself to come along. But how did he get in? The front doors were always locked. This was planned all along, and now I am going to be his victim.

He told me to take off my clothes.

How could he do this to me? I was so nice to him. I begged him not to hurt me.

Then he said, "I'm going to rape you, and then I'm going to kill you."

I saw the look in his eyes and knew he meant it. So, I did what he asked, but in the back of my mind I was going a million miles a minute, thinking of how to get out of this. The worst thing I could have told him was that I was still a virgin and saving myself for marriage, which is exactly the next thing I said. I was so beyond terrified, of course I said whatever popped into my head. I wasn't thinking clearly. Somehow, finding out I was still a virgin made me more of a prize. The second I told him, I could see pleasure in his eyes, like he really picked a good one. What a sick, disturbed individual he was.

The more I pleaded with him, the more he enjoyed it. I think he liked the power of holding my virginity and my life in his hands. I was standing in front of pure evil, desperately struggling to survive the biggest fight of my life. I think I may have had another out of body experience, or it was something I desperately wanted at the time.

I started to pray. I have never felt more scared in my entire life. I remember thinking death might be a blessing considering what he was doing to me. So totally gross. Such a violation and so very painful and violent. However, the will to live is stronger, and I was still so young and had so much I still wanted to live for. Was I really going to let this stranger take my life from me? No, I wasn't. Not even an option. My moment to strike came, and I knew I better make one shot count or I was dead.

I gathered up all the strength I had and I kicked him right in the nuts.

I mean, I kicked him hard, right square in the nuts. He immediately doubled over on the floor, moaning and rolling around. I wasted no time. I grabbed my clothes and booked out of there so fast. Honestly, I never knew I could move that fast. How I managed such accuracy with that one shot, I will never know. I have always felt that I had divine help. I had one chance or I was dead and I knew it. That one chance had to be completely accurate, and it sure was.

I ran to my friend Paul's room and pounded on his door. I wasn't even dressed yet, in a total state of panic, running through the dorm to find myself standing at my friend's door, totally naked with my clothes in my hands. It took me a while to get out what happened, and right when Paul heard me say the words, "I was raped," he ran out to get the guy.

It was too late. The guy was already gone.

Paul went upstairs to my friend Kelly's room to tell her what had happened and they both took me to the hospital. I was so hysterical I think Paul needed some support to help deal with me. The hospital was a dreadful, horrible experience. The nurse yelled at me to relax so they could do the exam. *Of course I'm tense lady! I was just raped, you ignorant burnout!* I hope nobody else in my situation ever gets treated like this. What a little compassion at that moment could have done to help. What was I expecting, kindness? That wasn't going to happen.

I was so incredibly bloody, too. My pants were soaked in blood. No counselor came into my hospital room to talk to me. No support from any of the medical staff whatsoever. Just a burned-out nurse yelling at me to relax.

I called out to my friends to come take me away. I got dressed in my disgusting clothes and we left. No, they didn't even keep my clothes as evidence. I have really no idea what the hospital even did that day besides yell at me to relax. How was that supposed to help? I didn't talk to a police officer either. Didn't they understand I was raped? Didn't they see all the blood? How are they not feeling any sympathy for me?

My dreams were already murdered, I just didn't know it yet. This began my endless effort to shower the incident off me. What I really wanted was to get new skin and throw this tainted one away. Maybe then I would feel clean. This was a brutal attack, and if this is what sex is about, then I want no part of it. I was also so brainwashed by my parents as to how bad, nasty, and evil sex is, and now I agree. It isn't a beautiful thing at all; it's a horrible, painful, evil, awful, disgusting thing.

I started to think I needed to quit school. It was a horrible time in my life. I was a virgin and he had a knife. Not anymore, I guess. How can someone, a total stranger, steal something so sacred? I can't emphasize enough: it was a brutal attack. I needed to move home. I was just too scared to stay in school. It was constantly on my mind. I couldn't concentrate on anything, especially school.

No matter how hard I tried, I couldn't get it out of my head. Every time I tried to walk through campus, I felt terrified, and I just couldn't do it any longer. I wanted to lock myself up somewhere isolated so I would be safe. I was starting to develop fears of anything and everything outside of what I considered safe, which was nothing and nowhere. I used to think I was safe in my dorm because the front doors were always locked. Evil still managed to get in, so where could I possibly be safe?

Sometimes I had to walk through campus alone, even at night. I would walk close to other groups of people just not to be alone. I was so terrified he would come back and kill me because I'd seen his face. I could identify him. *Maybe the horrible nightmares would go away if I move out of the building where my brutal attack took place?* The weird thing was, I couldn't remember what his face looked like. In every one of my horrible nightmares, all I could see was his blonde hair and his face was completely blacked out. No matter how hard I tried to see it, I just couldn't. To this day, once in a while I will have that terrible nightmare again and I still cannot see his face. I have absolutely no idea what he looked like.

He not only stole my virginity in a brutal way, he also killed my dream. I felt so angry at myself for allowing that to happen. I'd wanted that dream since I was eleven years old. Most of the time, though, I felt so darn scared and alone. I was afraid of everything, especially the nighttime. *How am I supposed to wake up every morning and function normally when this is the first thing I think about? How am I supposed to go to bed at night and sleep peacefully when this is the last thing I think about? I'm scared to death to close my eyes. How do people do this to other people? It doesn't seem real.*

I had the pain and scars to remind me it was real. The scars on my body healed after a while, but the scars on my soul are very much still there. I often wondered why I didn't fight back harder. I used to chastise myself and blame myself for the rape, which makes absolutely no sense in hindsight. I was living a life obsessed with what had happened to me yet not doing a thing to help myself. I didn't have a clue how to help myself.

There is so much now I wish I had done to help myself, but I lacked the self-esteem then. I refused to talk to anyone, even my closest friends, about it. Nobody knew what was wrong with me, but most people knew something was. However, I still had zero support.

I'm damaged now. I'm completely broken. I don't care because I don't want to get close to anybody, especially any man.

🙞 6 🙜

"Want to make God laugh? Tell him your plans." On a bumper sticker, it's laughable, but it's still not funny for the one making plans. I couldn't take it anymore, so I quit school. My dream, for now, was dead. Better than me being dead, but oh how depressing.

I will just go home, get myself together, and try again another day at another place, I thought. Right now, though, I just need to breathe. I need to go find a job and work for a while and just live my life as best I can.

Initially, I didn't tell my parents why I was quitting school. They thought I was quitting because I was just homesick, and I allowed them to think that. Dad was good enough to take a day off work and drive down to college to collect me and my belongings. In just two short weeks, I came to understand the cliché that you can't go back home. It was horrible. I needed to get out. I still had the same midnight curfew, and my mother was in control of me again. I was going through too much; I couldn't deal with her, too. I really hadn't thought much about what I would do when I moved home. All I knew was that I had to get away from college.

I had planned to find another school to study medicine at, but I needed time to get over the rape, if that were even possible. So, I started looking for a job. Dad said I should consider working in a bank, so I applied for a position at a new bank opening up in town. I interviewed and was hired on the spot. The branch manager must have had an idea of who he wanted as the face of the new location because when I met the other new employees, they all looked like me: young, attractive women. I wasn't hired on my abilities or my brain. Oh well. It was a job and it paid enough that I believed I could soon escape my parents' prison. I didn't exactly appreciate being objectified; however, it was a job and nothing near as tragic as the rape.

My boss was a little odd though. He who used to run his hands over the back of our tops to make sure we were wearing bras. If I showed up at work wearing pants, I was sent back home to put on a dress. I'm sure he should have been reported for sexual harassment; however, everyone just put up with it. After a while, he finally settled down and stopped.

This was a job with a group of people whom I would come to love. I always think about this as the best job I've ever had. We grew the business together, went out and partied at night together, and were there for each other like a close family. We even went door to door to let people know we were about to open a new bank.

After this job, I never worked at another place where everyone got along so well. I knew every angle of this job. No matter what the job, I always prided myself on doing it to the best of my ability. However, I wasn't allowed to be in management because I didn't have a college degree. This was a very strict rule of the banking industry back in the early '80s. *Stupid rule.* Were people really more qualified to be a manager just because they had graduated from a college? What about experience?

To add to what I felt was already an insult, I was assigned the task of training the people coming in out of college. Most of them didn't give a shit about what I was trying to teach them, and all I wanted to do was smack some sense into them on a regular basis.

I purchased my beautiful, sexy, bright yellow 280Z sports car when

THIS DOES NOT LEAVE THIS HOUSE

I worked here, all on my own, no co-signature needed from my father. I was very proud of my new independence and excited to show my father since he was a car enthusiast, too. He always had nice cars. Dad was outside when I pulled into their driveway. He asked me whose car I was driving. When I told him it was mine, he got really upset and told me to take it back. *Oh sure, Dad! How many times have you ever returned a car?* I hoped he would have been proud of me for doing this all on my own without having to ask him to cosign. However, my father was a major control freak, and I had taken this away from him. *I am an adult and a survivor now. I think I can handle buying a car.*

I swear, every police officer in town knew me and my bright yellow sports car. I didn't have a lot of cleavage to get out of all my speeding tickets, so I had to be creative every time I was pulled over. My favorite argument was, "Well, officer, this car is meant to be driven fast." Another one was, "I am doing an injustice to the car if I go slow, and it could damage the engine." *OK, Julie, here's your ticket!* I was better at speeding than getting out of a ticket. I got to know some pretty attractive police officers too. However, I was still afraid of all men, so, no thank you, not interested.

I rented a really cute condo on the golf course. I made the mistake of renting my extra bedroom to a customer I'd met at the bank. She was a studious person from Willamette University and most of the time she kept to herself. No social life here, unfortunately. She always shut herself up in her room and never wanted to talk to me except to yell at me when I threw a party. So, I suggested she move out. Good riddance. My friends were my love supply, and nobody was going to keep me away from them. Moral to this story is: know the person you are going to live with and know if you are compatible first, or it's going to be a miserable time.

My parties were pretty epic, too. The more the merrier was my slogan, and the party could last all night as far as I was concerned. Most of them did. Everybody came to my parties. I invited everyone I knew from high school and work to my parties—a few stragglers also, but I could count on my guy friends to police my parties. They called it "vag patrol," which stood for vagrant patrol. Usually, the boys ended up in one room playing poker and the girls in another room gossiping. As long as there was plenty of booze in the kitchen, everyone was happy.

One of the best parties I ever threw was at my friend Kathy's house back when we were still in high school. I practically lived at her house. Her bedroom was in the basement with a door leading outside of the house, which we used frequently to sneak out. Her parents were fond of leaving for the entire weekend, so we had time to party. What kid wouldn't love this arrangement? Especially a sheltered one like me, who had zero freedom. I can attest truth to the stereotype about kids like me who tend to go a little crazy when they are allowed a little freedom.

Kathy and I filled the bathtub with ice and beer and planned to collect fees at the door to pay for all of it, but once a few people came, we got busy socializing and forgot to collect any money. Oh well, that was the best party ever. Lasted two entire days. Everyone stayed to help us clean it all up before her parents got home. Everyone was out, the house was clean, and her parents arrived about ten minutes later. We never cared that it had cost a fortune either. My friends were everything to me and keeping them around me and happy was everything too.

One Saturday night, my closest girlfriends and I were in my beautiful condo on the golf course watching *Fantasy Island*. Saturday nights back then were reserved for *Love Boat* and *Fantasy Island*, and I rarely missed them. We were spread out all over the front room, and some of the girls were sitting on the stairs with me. So, the *Fantasy Island* story this week was about a mermaid who fell in love with a mortal man. Finally, at the end, the mortal man decided not to turn into a merman and join the mermaid. The mermaid was heartbroken. It was all very sad.

My friends Rosie and Kathy cried, "Oh no! What will the mermaid do now?"

I answered, grinning, "She's going to go find Moby Dick!"

Betsy laughed so hard she rolled off the stairs. Good times with the girls!

I have no patience for people who think their "shit" is ice cream.

You know, those people who think they are superior to everyone else. I don't like entitled or stuck-up people. Never have. Never will. One day at the bank, a wealthy male customer came up to my window to conduct a transaction. When I asked him for identification he got very upset.

"Don't you know who I am?" His attitude caught me off-guard. "I only own half of Salem."

"Oh yeah?" I retorted, bravely. "You should know me too, then."

He looked at me, perplexed.

"Why is that?"

I looked him straight in the eye.

"Because I own the other half."

Shut him the hell up.

Yes, there were people in my town who had a lot of money, and they were all pretty much losers that had gotten it all from daddy. Make your own fortune and then you can brag. Otherwise, shut the hell up.

I have always been a strong believer in donating blood, especially when the blood drive is at the US Bank where all the cute boys worked. I sat down on a cot and started giving blood completely surrounded by cute boys. No kidding, they hired male models at this bank. I was doing really well until a nurse walked up to me and started squishing my blood bag in her hands. I looked at my own blood and immediately started hyperventilating. I felt someone quickly lower my head, lift my feet up, then make me breathe into a paper bag. *So embarrassing.* The sad thing is, even if one of these cute boys had asked me out, I wouldn't have accepted. I was doing everything in my power not to deal with the rape, and the last thing in the world I could deal with was dating.

Things were going a bit better in my life since the rape, but I still had this nagging fear and some depression I was trying to drink, socialize, and party away. I got a DUII two weeks after I turned twenty-one. What happened next added even more confusion to my ongoing distress.

This story is so bizarre . . .

I was stopped at a stop light and a guy in a car next to us was trying really hard to get our attention. He was obviously drunk, too. So, the light turns green and we start to go; however, we didn't know a police officer was behind us. Without stopping, he directed me through his loudspeaker to pull over as he went after the other car. I did as he said. I was a good girl and sat there and waited for him to come back and arrest me. He was at least two blocks away, I probably should have just left, but I didn't have the nerve to do that. I was dumb enough to drive after drinking, but I wasn't a complete lawbreaker.

My friend kept telling me we should take off, but I waited too long and the officer came back. The guy from the other car was sitting in the back seat of the police car. The officer didn't even handcuff me. He told me I was under arrest and let me sit in the front seat of the car next to him. I thought my girlfriend was more inebriated than I was, but he instructed her to drive my car to the police station. I was booked and released and the police officer told me to have my friend drive us home. *OK, but shouldn't we get a ride or call a cab?* I was worried it was a set-up and he would be waiting around the corner to arrest my friend, but he wasn't.

We had been back at my house for only about an hour when I heard a knock at the door. By then it was four in the morning. I opened the door and the police officer who arrested me was standing there. He said he forgot to write down my license plate and was there to get it. *What?* I thought that was really strange and was glad my friend was still there. I found it fishy that he'd forgotten to write down the license plate. I figured that is probably one of the first things they do when they pull you over. The whole thing seemed creepy. What were the officer's intentions? I am sure they weren't good. I couldn't imagine how I would have survived another rape. Who would have believed me?

The next day I went to see a girlfriend whose husband was a very respected attorney in town. I met with him, and he agreed to take on my case. Too bad he knew my Uncle John, who was also an attorney in town. He decided to call my Uncle John and tell him about my DUII. My uncle immediately called my parents and told them what happened. My uncle also convinced my friend's husband to let him handle my case. Even when I had tried to handle something on my own, it got screwed up. I was extremely upset because I didn't want my parents to know about my DUI. I wanted to handle it myself, but here I go again. How dare the attorney call my Uncle and tell him about my DUI. Wasn't that a breach of client-attorney privilege? However, I was really good friends with his wife and didn't want to stir up any trouble. *Oh goodie, more ammunition for my dear, sweet mother.*

Of course, my mother used this as an excuse to bad-mouth me again. She relished in telling everyone in the family I was an alcoholic. I wasn't an alcoholic, just a stupid kid who drank too much one night, made a stupid choice to drive, and got pulled over. *Thanks for the support, Mom.* To this day, I believe she still sees me in this light. I'm sure most of my family still think I'm an alcoholic. I don't drink alcohol because of my bad pancreas—my pancreas is damaged from a gallstone, not from alcohol—but they all must think it's because I'm an alcoholic. *I have got to stop giving my mother ammunition to use against me.* She thrived on it. She loved when she had something negative to spread about me. What kind of mother does this? Certainly not a loving one.

Besides, my mother isn't really one to talk. When I was seventeen, my dad was out of town on a buying trip for the men's clothing store he managed. I invited a boy I had just barely started dating over to our house for dinner. I made some strawberry daiquiris at Mom's request, even though my date and I weren't of age. Mom proceeded to get wasted. We were all sitting at the kitchen table when Mom decided she wanted to sit on my new boyfriend's lap. I was mortified. I didn't know what to say. She was all over this boy in no time, spilled her ashtray in his lap, and kept calling him "lover." *Seriously, flirting with my boyfriend now, Mother?* So completely embarrassing and no, he never asked me out again.

I remember another time I was dating a boy from a very rich family who owned an insurance company. Mom decided she didn't like him. My parents hired a private investigator to follow me and my boyfriend for reasons I am still not sure of. Since his parents worked in the insurance industry, they knew the private investigator my parents hired because he already worked for them. The investigator thought the ethical thing to do was to inform my boyfriend's parents that he was recently hired by my parents. His parents were angered and appalled at what my parents had done. I never understood why they did it, and they never gave me a reason either. To me, it felt like such an invasion and such a betrayal. Another relationship, once again, ended because of my mother.

7

I was asleep one night in my condo by the golf course when I had an incredible dream. It was so vivid. In my dream, I was out of my body watching myself get out of bed and walk down the stairs. I had heard a knock at my door and was going down to answer it. All of a sudden, as I was opening my front door, I was back in my body again. My precious Grandma Eva was at my door.

Grandma said, "Take my hand." I gave her my hand and I instantly felt warm and comforted. I had the sense she was really there in spirit, so I was surprised when my hand didn't go through hers. We walked through the condo parking lot. She held my hand the entire time.

Grandma told me, "I am always here with you, watching over you. Everything is going to be OK. I know you are going through a very hard time right now, but you are going to get through it."

I told her, "Grandma, I miss you terribly and I really need you." Grandma assured me she had been with me every step of the way.

The last thing Grandma said to me was, "I am very proud of the young lady you are becoming. You will recover because you still have work to do here on this earth."

She walked me back to my condo, turned around, and walked away.

As I watched her walk away, she appeared to be surrounded by pure light and then, all of a sudden, she disappeared.

It was a very pleasant, peaceful dream that I never wanted to wake up from. I was surprised when she assured me she had never left me. She always watches over me. What a warm and contented feeling that gave me. I woke up from this dream knowing I had been with her. This wasn't just a dream at all.

The very next day I drove over to my parents' house so I could tell my father about my dream. He turned a bit white when I shared some details. *She was wearing a beautiful brocade jacket and matching skirt. It was shiny material and light blue in color. Her hair was perfectly curled, and she was wearing black patent leather high heels. She wore a crystal brooch on the right side of her jacket.* He told me that I had just described what she was buried in, right down to her brooch.

Remember, I wasn't allowed to attend her funeral. This was no dream at all. I had been visited by Grandma Eva. She really looked radiant and beautiful. I was told this was the outfit she'd worn when she had married her second husband, Bill. I will not discuss him at all. He was a horrible, mean man and wasn't kind to my sweet grandma. To this day, I cherish this visit and think of it often.

It took me a year to finally tell my family about the rape. I told my brother first. He was in a band at the time, and I went to watch him perform at a place in Eugene called "Tavern on the Green." They were very good, and I figured they were headed for stardom. But his music career was short-lived. His band had a disagreement shortly after that performance and broke up.

That night, he sat down with me during a break. I'd had a couple glasses of wine and got up enough nerve to tell him why I'd really left college. He actually cried a little bit. He said he'd let me down because he was supposed to be there to protect me. I assured him there was nothing he could have done. This was the first time anyone ever shed a tear for me.

My brother couldn't believe I hadn't told our parents yet. He thought it was important that I tell them, and he even came with me to support me while I told them.

"You're lying," the words came from my mother. "That never happened."

At that moment, I wished I had never said a word. *Are you kidding me? How in the world do you sit there and accuse me of lying? Don't you get it? It took me an entire year and a lot of encouragement to tell you about this. You suck so much, Mom. You really do. Why was I given a piece of shit mother like you?*

"Let's get out of here." I could hear the frustration in my brother's voice.

I left feeling so hurt. I had zero support from my parents.

My parents never talked to me about it after that night. Subject dropped, disappeared, doesn't exist. Swept under the carpet. I vowed to never share another part of my life with them. She accuses me of lying and, as usual, my father just sits there and says nothing. *Nothing!* I just know Mom is going to find a way to gossip about me to everyone who will listen about this, and she did. She took my deepest wound and found a way to use it against me. She tried to make everyone look at me like I had done something wrong. Why do I keep giving her ammunition? Why do I keep giving her ways to mock me?

Well, here you go, Mom, on a silver platter, knock yourself out.

❧ 8 ❧

I worked in banking for about five years and had pretty much given up on my dream to be a doctor. However, what about nursing? I believed nurses could do a lot of good. As long as they aren't mean, stupid, snarky, or burned-out lunatics, like the one who treated me after I was raped.

Our community college had a great nursing program. I applied and was accepted. Nursing school was tough. Nothing for me came easily, but I knew how to do the work. I always got good grades as a result.

My friends and I had a local haunt called O'Callahan's. We loved going there because all our friends from high school hung out there and they had a different live band performing every weekend. I met a new friend there named Kathy through one of my other friends. We became instant bar friends. She asked me one night at O'Callahan's if I wanted to meet a nice guy.

I told her, "No thanks. Nice guys don't exist."

She walked me over to this guy standing at the bar, very drunk and wearing a brown leather coat and a baseball hat.

"His name is Steve," she said, "and he's my brother."

He was so drunk he could barely stand up. We all went to a party after the bar closed and Steve came along too. He was too drunk for conversation that night, but he eventually called and asked me out for a date. I seriously don't remember where we went or what we did. Knowing him, it probably involved a bar.

Five years had been long enough to abstain from men, and I needed to get back out there, all my friends agreed. Besides that, I thought he was really cute. Steve's interests were hunting, fishing, and drinking beer. None of these things interested me. He drank way too much and occasionally smoked marijuana. I hated marijuana. It changed Steve and made him angry. He experimented with other drugs later. He was a good-looking guy that all the girls wanted. This is probably the biggest reason I was attracted to him. We really had nothing in common. He could be very nice and funny when sober, but he became a different person when he was drunk.

I had to tread very carefully around him when he was drunk and not say the wrong thing to him. Still, I guess most of the time I really liked him, so I overlooked the little flaws. He could be very charming and a lot of fun to be around. Later, those little flaws became big problems.

I found out I was pregnant when I was twenty-five. Steve and I had dated for two years by then, but we weren't married and no talk of marriage had come up yet. I was on birth control pills but quite possibly missed one or two. When I saw that plus symbol on the pregnancy test, I couldn't believe what I was looking at. I just sat and stared at it for the longest time in disbelief.

My thoughts were racing: *I am almost done with nursing school. Only two terms from becoming a nurse. I'm pregnant? Oh Lord! I'm not ready to be a mom. I want to be a mom someday, but this is quite possibly the very worst timing ever.*

I started to panic. *I had some drinks the other night. Is that going to hurt the baby? My boyfriend smokes pot. Is that going to hurt the baby?*

I never once thought of the possibility of terminating the pregnancy. Worst timing, yes, but the thought of being a mom made me so happy. I think the second I knew I was pregnant I felt drawn to my baby and felt an instant need to protect.

When I told Steve, he insisted on an abortion. If I refused, he said he would leave me. I refused. His next move was to take the TV he had previously purchased out of my apartment. *Was this my punishment?* He was so angry that I was defying him he made a fist and threatened to hit me in the stomach so I would lose the baby. When I yelled at him to get the hell away from me, he simply turned and left. This was the last time I would ever yell at him and not get hit for it.

So, there I sat. It was a Saturday night, no TV, and my 280Z was broken down in the parking lot. I was completely alone. I sat on the couch patting my stomach and telling my baby not to worry. I would always be there.

I was born to be a mother. I have always wanted to be one, but this is not how I wanted it to happen. The timing is terrible. Oh well, I obviously was chosen for this, so I better make the best of it. Here comes the fun part: telling my parents.

I drove to their house a few days later and broke the news to them. In their very special way, they completely freaked out. They took my car keys and wouldn't let me leave their house. This was pretty typical of them when they were angry at me: hold me hostage until they are done hammering on me. I was there for three hours while my parents yelled at me about what a horrible slut I was and how I needed to get rid of the baby.

I remember thinking to myself, *If you think I am such a slut, you don't even know me at all.* Remember my rape? It took me years to be comfortable with anyone after my rape, and now I'm some kind of slut? Had they forgotten they were Catholic? *Strict Catholics, too,* I thought. Are they changing the rules? Maybe the rules only work when it's convenient for them. They suggested I go live in a convent in another state until the baby was born and then give it up for adoption. They also came up with an idea for me to go live with some family members in California. They were desperate to get me away from them so I wouldn't embarrass them or tarnish the family's perfect reputation. It was 1985, not 1955. I was an adult, not a pregnant teen. I refused all of their ridiculous suggestions and finally got the hell out of there.

Again . . . thanks for all the support, Mom and Dad. You're the best! Now give me back my damn car keys.

A few days later, my mother called me to say she had made me an appointment with her ob/gyn doctor, the same one who had delivered my brother and me. I was really happy that finally my parents had come around and accepted the fact that I was pregnant. *Finally, I am getting a little support.* I felt somewhat suspicious but told myself to try to put the past in the past and move forward. *Maybe they are trying.*

"We don't do abortions at this office." The doctor had just finished the exam.

What?

"We'll have to send you up to Portland."

I couldn't believe what I was hearing.

"I am not here for an abortion. I thought this was my first pregnancy visit. Don't you need to give me some prenatal vitamins or something?"

I am not here for an abortion!

The doctor didn't answer and I realized what was happening. My mother had made me an appointment for an abortion. *How completely, outrageously despicable.* They could have started the abortion process without me even knowing it and then it would have been too late.

Mom, you blew it! Now until forever you will have nothing to do with me and my child.

She tried to kill my baby against my will. *Who does this stuff? Could this be considered attempted murder?* I decided to have nothing to do with my parents and committed myself to going through this completely alone. *It's OK if I have no support.*

To recap, Steve almost punched me in the stomach to make me lose my baby. My mother tried to trick me into an abortion, and my father tried to send me away to a convent in California. In other words, no support whatsoever and no new baby fanfare. I was disowned and abandoned soon after announcing the big news. *I need to be strong for my child and move past all this craziness.*

Later, I found out her doctor was so enraged by what my mother had tried to do to me that he fired her in his office that same day despite the fact she had been his patient for over thirty years. He referred me to another gynecologist because he was retiring. I set out to make it on my own, without my parents or my baby's father.

I adored my new doctor. He took excellent care of me throughout the pregnancy. I did everything I was told and took really good care of myself. I instantly stopped smoking and took the prenatal vitamins even though they made me sick. After my first trimester, I felt better than at any other time in my life. Weigh-in days at the doctor's sent me straight to the ice cream parlor for a hot fudge sundae. I am normally very small, yet I had gotten so big that people were constantly asking me if I were having twins. I joked, "I've got one in my stomach and one in my butt."

At five-foot-almost-two-inches tall, I weighed over two hundred pounds when Stephanie was born. She weighed a whopping six pounds, nine ounces. I was so stressed out all the time that the weight fell right off.

Yet again, I somehow found a way to forgive my mother, and we moved on with life. A few years later, however, she did something to me so far beyond forgiveness and so toxic that I had to finally let her go forever.

Steve and I ended up getting married under pressure from my father. It was nothing like I had always imagined my wedding would be. Supposed to be an exciting time? Bridal shower in Vegas? Well, not for me. No glamour, no fanfare. Not even a bridal shower. Mom and Dad shopped with me for a wedding dress. I could still hear Mom's voice in my head as she insisted, "Don't you dare think about wearing a white wedding gown since you are already pregnant."

My Grandma Eva had made me a Barbie wedding gown when I was a little girl. I played with it for hours, dreaming of my own wedding dress. This certainly wasn't it. This was not going to be a joyous occasion. This was going to be a wedding of embarrassment and punishment, brought to you by my loving parents. My wedding day would be my penance for getting knocked up. *I feel like I have been here before.* So, we picked out a pink dress. Someone else with a backbone would have fought for what they had always dreamed of. Not me. I was ashamed and trying to please everyone else.

The wedding took place in the basement of Steve's grandparents' house. This was OK with me. I just wanted to get it over with. My brother even came from Los Angeles with his latest girlfriend du jour. She was gorgeous. They all were. I felt fat and ugly and a total embarrassment to my family. The only thing I remember about my wedding day was my brother's girlfriend coming into my room to try to help me look a little "more pretty." *Does anyone have a gun?*

We honeymooned at the beach in Lincoln City, Oregon. Steve got his hands on a bottle of champagne and drank it in the bathtub. *Interesting choice*, I thought. Why would he choose to drink it alone in the bathtub? He didn't invite me to join him and I was good with that. I was so exhausted that I just wanted to be left alone. He passed out in the tub.

The only thing about our honeymoon I had been looking forward to was our dinner reservations at Ricardo's Fish House. It wasn't easy to find. The beach didn't have many fancy restaurants. All Steve seemed to care about was whether he had enough money for alcohol. He didn't care that I was pregnant and needed to eat. He also refused to take his baseball cap off during dinner even though we were in a fancy place. He got so angry at me for picking such an expensive restaurant that was going to cut into his alcohol allotment. This is all I can remember of my honeymoon.

By the time I found out I was pregnant, I only had two terms left in nursing school. I ended up quitting school. I didn't feel like I had a choice. I needed to get a job to earn more money for the baby and never went back. I never became a nurse. Life doesn't turn out exactly how we imagine it does it?

I found a job at a mortgage loan office. When I started to show, I told the other girl in the office that I was going to have a baby. She was very happy for me and very supportive. However, the boss wasn't so happy. He called me into his office one day and told me he was talking with corporate to find a way that he could "legally" fire me. I couldn't believe it. He said he didn't want to deal with me being on maternity leave. He was a horrible person who made me feel horrible and he treated his staff, well, horribly. After Stephanie was born, I didn't go back to work there. I never wanted to be in an uncomfortable situation where I wasn't wanted. I had no choice as a child, but I am an adult now, so no thanks.

Steve didn't make much money at his job and thought he might have better luck moving to Dallas, Oregon. Steve had grown up in

Dallas, had worked in Dallas, and he wanted to move to back to Dallas. I didn't want to move there, but I succumbed because he wanted it so badly. He wouldn't stop talking about it, whining about it, arguing about it, and, after a while, it got so annoying that I just gave in. I was used to giving in to people when they got upset or whiny. Turned out to be one of the worst decisions of my life.

I wasn't aware of this at the time, but most everyone in that little town hated me. A couple years before getting pregnant, Kathy, Steve's sister, invited me to go barhopping with her in Portland. I didn't want to go, and something in my gut strongly told me not to. Steve and Kathy convinced me to go, so I went.

Kathy offered to be the designated driver and swore to me she was only going to drink water. Shortly after we left the bar, she lost control of the car and we wrecked on the freeway onramp. Luckily for us, we didn't leave the road and go sliding down a big embankment. We just spun around a bunch of times and I ended up in the back seat of her car.

Somehow, she managed to drive to a convenience store parking lot. We called her mother in Dallas to come get us. This was weird: the convenience store was closed. Don't convenience stores stay open twenty-four hours? It was around two in the morning when we got there. Scary-looking people were walking around too.

We got out of the car to use the pay phone next to the store. A couple of sketchy looking guys pulled up, came over to us, and asked if we wanted any drugs. The car had broken down as soon as we'd parked it, so we were very polite when we said no. We sat there scared for an hour and a half waiting for her mother to arrive.

We were on our way back to Dallas when I requested they take me to the hospital in Salem. I was beginning to have a lot of pain from a couple of broken bones and a really bad headache. I was diagnosed with a severe concussion. I was referred to a neurologist to be evaluated.

I remember one visit my father took me to. As the concussion progressed, I lost my ability to speak. Everything was coming out garbled and unrecognizable. My loving mother would tell me, "Don't talk. You sound like a retard." I remember sitting there listening while the doctor proceeded to tell my father they might need to drill a hole in my head to let the pressure out. I definitely had an opinion about this, but, since I couldn't talk very well, I couldn't express it. Luckily, they didn't have to resort to those measures and I eventually recovered.

Anyway, her insurance company refused to pay my medical bills because I refused to sign their medical release form. I was advised by my uncle, the lawyer in the family, not to sign their medical release forms. This decision caused me so many problems and hate from his family and their friends, which was pretty much all of Dallas. I was only doing what I was advised to do by someone I thought at the time had my best interest in mind.

I am moving to a town where everyone hates me. I just don't know it yet. I will soon enough. Things are about to get ugly. I have enough on my plate right now. I will deal with this later.

❧ 9 ❧

I had a dream about my baby two weeks before she was born. I was holding a baby girl in a pink receiving blanket, and someone asked me what my baby's name was. I answered, "Stephanie." I woke up thinking that was weird since everyone predicted I was going to have a boy. We never found out the sex. I wanted to be surprised.

When she was born and the doctor said, "It's a girl!" I immediately said, "Stephanie." She even looked exactly the same way she did in my dream. I got a glimpse into what my daughter looked like two weeks before she came into this world. As excited as I had been about Stephanie's arrival, I was terrified to go through labor. When the time finally came, I turned into a screaming thing out of a B-rated horror movie. My labor was horrible. I had to be induced two weeks before the due date because I had toxemia. The drug used to induce was called Pitocin, and it works quickly. Labor begins right away with absolutely no breaks. The pain was incredible. I laid in my hospital bed pleading and begging for something to relieve the pain. It was over 100 degrees outside that day too. A broken air conditioning unit in my hospital room meant it was almost as warm inside. They were at full capacity and didn't have another room available. I was drenched in sweat and in pain like I'd never experienced before in my life.

However, when they finally got around to bringing me a pain shot, I had almost completely dilated and the pain was actually a little better. Out of protest for them making me wait, I decided to turn it down. I don't think the nurse was too pleased with me as she stood there holding a pain shot in her hand, looking at me like I'm a complete lunatic. I decided I had come this far without it and I could go the distance without it. I prided myself on getting through the entire labor with nothing for pain.

After hours of labor, Stephanie arrived. They let me hold her for the first time, and I couldn't believe what I saw. My baby was perfect and so beautiful. I couldn't stop crying. I held her for what felt like a very short time when they took her away. They said they needed to test her for different things and weigh her and stuff like that. I felt such an incredible feeling of separation anxiety that continued to follow me for the first few months of her life.

Because my baby was now away from me, the nurse insisted I get up to shower. I told her I was way too weak, but she insisted. As soon as I stood up, I passed out, blood gushing out of me. I awoke to two or three nurses pushing their fists into my stomach to stop the bleeding. When it finally did and the nurses left the room, I was exhausted and starving. One nurse returned with a sandwich for me. My husband ate half of it.

The nurse yelled, "You can go get anything you want anywhere. This is all she gets right now."

I got a lot of satisfaction watching this. What an idiot. He had slept during the majority of the time I was in labor. How he did that is beyond me. *Hungover again?* What a worthless piece of shit.

Stephanie was born at 8:30 in the evening. I was finally placed in a cooler room a little before midnight. Back in the '80s, they didn't believe in putting babies in the room with the mothers. They were kept in the nursery. I was having intense separation anxiety being away from my baby. Instead of calling for a nurse, I got out of bed and walked up the long hallway to the nursery. I was so weak. I had to lean on the wall just to get to the end of the hallway. I knocked on the window and a nurse came out and immediately put me in a wheelchair. She was so shocked to see me.

"What are you doing out of bed?"

I burst into tears. "I want my baby," I cried.

She pushed me back to my room, got me back in bed, and left, returning in just a few moments with my baby. She placed her in my arms, and that is where she stayed all night long.

I couldn't take my eyes off her.

I was beyond exhausted by this time but so taken by my beautiful girl. I didn't sleep at all that night. It was our first night together, just me and my precious Stephanie. Her father left right after the sandwich incident. I guess he needed to go home and get some rest. He only returned when it was visiting hours.

You don't exactly sleep well in the hospital between the nurses coming in every hour, the visitors, and just the sheer amazement at becoming a new mommy. After three days, I went home feeling sleep-deprived but ready to care for my baby, who didn't necessarily care if she slept through the night and needed to eat every two hours around the clock.

She wanted nothing to do with breastfeeding. This one time I tried to breastfeed her, she wrinkled up her nose and looked at me as if to say, "You've got to be kidding me." She had attitude already and I loved it. I think all girls need to have a little sass to get them through life. I was going to give her everything I always wished I had, and heaven knows I could have used a little more sass.

I wasn't too keen on breastfeeding either, so we went with formula. We didn't own a microwave, nor could we afford one, so I heated up her bottle in a pot of water on the stove. Yes, it took forever. Try that one time with a baby screaming your ear off. I didn't mind for myself, but I couldn't stand to see her unhappy. I just gently bounced her while we waited and hoped I could calm her.

During her two-in-the-morning feedings, we watched MTV music videos. Back in the '80s, MTV was only music videos, and they weren't very good videos either. The same darn videos played every morning at 2 a.m. too. Trust me, I was up. The one I remember the most was "Two of Hearts" by Stacey Q. I remember she had big hair and jumped around a lot. I will forever remember this song fondly because it represented to me my quiet time alone with my girl.

Most of the time it was just me and Stephanie. Her father wasn't ready to be a dad. He worked nights and slept during the day. I talked him into giving Stephanie a bottle only one time, and I don't have a memory of him ever changing a diaper. When he had any spare time, it was spent hunting, fishing, drinking, and chasing tail in the bars of the small town we lived in. I remember when I was about eight months pregnant, our home phone rang. There were no cell phones back then. There was a woman on the other end.

"May I speak with Steve?" the voice inquired casually.

"Who is this?" I was annoyed. "What do you want?"

"I met him at the bar and he gave me this number and told me to call anytime," she answered.

"Do you know you're talking to his pregnant wife right now?"

She really didn't seem to care at all about that.

"Just tell him I called." She hung up.

What Mensa genius gives some chick they just met in a bar their home phone number where their wife is the one who most likely will be answering it? That was one message that was never passed on. I never said a word either. By this time, I was already somewhat afraid of him since he had already started abusing me. It's a weirdly scary feeling to be afraid of the person you married and who vowed to love you.

There aren't enough words to express the love I have always had from the very beginning for my Stephanie. It wasn't until much later that I realized she played a huge part in saving my life. It was primarily because of Stephanie that I got the strength to leave my abusive marriage. There was also another song back then that expressed my feeling for Stephanie perfectly. It was sung by Helen Reddy and called "You and Me Against the World." It would have been nice to have had a little help once in a while, but I was loving being a new mommy.

I was content being a mom. I felt my life now had meaning. I vowed to always give her love and teach her to have a high self-esteem and self-confidence. I told her every day many times how much she was loved. Everything I always wished I had, I showered on Stephanie. She was the perfect change in my life when I needed it the most.

I grew up fast after she was born. I felt the responsibility of it all immediately. I had a purpose, someone who depended entirely on me, and I was never going to let her down. I was still suffering with serious separation anxiety. The night we brought her home from the hospital, my lovely mom decided to invite the entire family over to our tiny townhouse for spaghetti. I just wanted to be alone. I was so exhausted, and the minute Stephanie was out of my sight and being passed around, I started to cry. This gave my mom her perfect opportunity to make fun of me, call me weak, and say cruel things about me, but it got my baby back in my arms and that was all I cared about.

Things were going really well, and, at only two weeks old, Stephanie slept through the night for the first time. *Scared me to death!* I woke up, looked at the clock, and it was 7:30 in the morning. I immediately woke her up, trying to make sure she was still breathing. That became a habit. I frequently woke this poor child making sure she was breathing. I was also a really paranoid new mom. I had this constant fear that something terrible was going to happen to her. I passed it off as new-mama jitters most of the time. Her well-baby check-up went perfectly. I had a healthy and happy baby on my hands—until she turned three weeks old, exactly to the day.

Stephanie was acting somewhat lethargic and she had a different cry. It sounded to me like she cried like she hurt. Even though I was still a new mom, I knew my baby, and I knew her different cries. My baby was in pain.

I called her pediatrician and he told me to give her some baby Tylenol and lay her down in her crib. I thought, *No way. This is serious. You are not going to treat me like a paranoid new mother and pass me off on some stupid Tylenol.* I had heard good things about another doctor in town and he even had his own local TV show. It was around 8 p.m. and after-hours by the time I called. I lied to his answering service and pretended Stephanie was a patient of his. I explained her symptoms to them and the doctor called me right back. He said he would meet me at the hospital emergency room.

Of course, again on my own, I drove her to the hospital, scared to death something was terribly wrong with my baby. I met Dr. Lace for the first time in the hospital emergency room. At first glance, in my opinion, he didn't look like a doctor at all. His hair was disheveled and he was wearing dirty corduroy pants. He resembled something more of a farmer than a doctor. However, I instantly trusted him. He ran his hand over the top of Stephanie's head and said her fontanel was swollen. What is a fontanel? It's the soft spot on top of babies' heads that isn't grown over with skull yet. In her case, it looked like her brain was swelling. He mentioned an illness he suspected she had called Spinal Meningitis and it was serious.

Can I please go back to being a paranoid new mom? Seriously, she is only three weeks old. How can she possibly fight this? Is this really happening? Could I be dreaming this perhaps?

Nope, not a dream. This *is* really happening. I rode up the elevator with Doctor Lace to the area where they were going to do a spinal tap to test if it was viral or bacterial meningitis. I wasn't allowed in the area where they were doing the spinal tap, but when I heard my baby cry, I collapsed onto the floor. My whole body just sank down the wall and onto the floor.

This is way more than I can handle. Please, Lord, make it go away.

A very kind, gentle nurse came over to me and helped me up, gave me some tissues, and told me to pull it together. She said, "Mama, get it together. Your baby needs you." At that moment, I became Super-mom. Bless that woman for giving me exactly what I needed at that exact moment. I never saw her again, but her words got me through some very rough times at the hospital. Preliminary tests came back. It was meningitis. We had to wait three days to find out if it was viral or bacterial.

I was told, "If your baby lives, she could be brain damaged, deaf, or both."

What?

All I could hear was, "If your baby lives."

We were placed in a pediatrics unit isolation room. Meningitis is highly contagious. I was supposed to wear a gown and a mask to protect me against it. I had no problem with the gown, but I just couldn't wear the mask around my baby. I was afraid it would scare her. So, much to the disdain of the nurses, I never wore a mask. I also rarely left my girl.

They put a rocking chair in the room next to the horrible sterile metal crib. Somehow, I instinctively knew that if I laid her down, she would lose her will to live. The only time I laid her down on that sterile crib was when I needed to change her diaper. Otherwise, she was always being held. When I had to run to the bathroom, I called a nurse in to hold her for me. I just sat there holding her in my arms, just my baby and me, alone in that rocking chair day and night, for five days.

On day three, the tests came back. She had the viral strain, not bacterial. I sat there and cried while I watched them unhook the antibiotic medicine they were giving her to fight it. Since it was viral, there was nothing they could do. No medicine was going to help her. I prayed harder than I had ever prayed in my entire life. I begged, pleaded, offered up myself instead of her, and made all kinds of deals. I think God got so tired of hearing from me he healed her just to shut me up. What I didn't realize at the time was that the viral strain was better to get than bacterial. All I'd heard was, "There's nothing more we can do," and that was so terrifying.

Imagine this: you just had a baby and you are still getting all your hormones back to normal. You've only had three weeks with your new baby, and now you are at risk of losing her. I've had some pretty bad times in my life, but this was the absolute worst.

Steve came to the hospital one time, the night his parents came by during visiting hours. He was there an entire hour and was gone again. I decided while I sat there late one night in that lonely isolation room that I was going to leave him. What was I staying for? I was alone anyway, and if I left him at least I wouldn't have to worry about getting hit anymore. My plan was set into motion.

After three nights in isolation, Stephanie's fever shot up over 105 degrees. They had to pack her in ice to get her fever down. The nurses told me high fevers are what can cause brain damage. I had never had a fever that high even with my worst kidney infection. I had never heard of anyone ever having a fever that high. This scared me to death. They also told me that my sweet little baby hadn't developed a lot of immunities yet. *It's because I hadn't breast-fed her. It was my fault she was so sick.*

Luckily, they were able to get her fever down quickly. The fourth night we were there was a Friday night. I was sleeping in the rocking chair, holding Stephanie in my lap. Early Saturday morning around three, a security guard came looking for me. We were still in isolation, but we were finally out of the woods and would be discharged soon. When the security guard found me, he asked, "What are you doing here?"

I said, "I'm here because my baby is sick."

"All the other parents look at us as their babysitters," he told me, "so they can go out and party on Friday nights."

Not this mother.

"Is that your yellow 280Z in the parking lot?"

"Yes, it is."

"I regret to inform you that all your windows have been busted out." He was so casual about it.

"All my windows are gone?" I couldn't believe what I was hearing.

"Yep," he said. "Smashed out with a baseball bat."

He thought it was perhaps a case of mistaken identity. Someone was really angry at someone else who owned a yellow 280Z and targeted the wrong car, which just happened to be my car. That said, they needed me to get my car out of there so they could clean up the glass that was all over the parking lot before the morning rush.

I called my father and told him what happened. I needed to bring my car to their house, and I needed him to get me right back to the hospital. Poor dad. He always had to clean up my messes. I found a nurse who could spare the time and stay with Stephanie so I could take care of this.

Really, universe? I am a new mom, alone with her sick baby in pediatrics, and some crazy person has just bashed in all my car windows?

All that mattered was getting back as fast as I could to my baby in the hospital. There wasn't time to feel sorry for myself, but I was heartbroken. I really loved this car. The security guard wasn't kidding: not one single window was spared. Oh well, cars can be fixed, and I have bigger problems right now. Man, that drive to my parents was so cold!

To this day, I consider my girl a miracle. She made a complete and full recovery. Of course, as a teenager she had the selective hearing they all do at that age. She was a very smart girl, too. The teachers wanted to put her in advanced placement classes. However, she tested right on the cusp. I decided against it. I always felt that socialization was just as important, and I didn't want them to do anything that isolated her even a little from the other children. I know there were other children in AP classes, too, but I never had a good experience being different in school, and I didn't want to risk that with Stephanie.

Another reason I consider her to be a miracle is because I was told I would never be able to carry a child due to all the kidney problems I'd had since I was two. I guess I am somewhat of a miracle myself. I was fifteen when I had my last kidney attack. That was when I almost died and had my out-of-body experience. Nobody in the medical field has been able to explain to me why I never had another kidney infection since then. I was told that I would need kidney dialysis someday and eventually a kidney transplant. I believe I was healed that day up in the corner of that room. I don't remember anything other than floating there. However, I felt the spirits around me even though I couldn't see them. It was truly a beautiful and magical experience.

One person who had helped me the most when Stephanie was in the hospital was my Aunt Jeannine. I have always adored her. She was so kind to me, and even though she was my mother's sister, she was nothing like her. She was caring and considerate, not mean and selfish like my mom. She knew I was going through a lot and hadn't had any sleep, so one Saturday she just showed up and told me to go get some rest. She stayed with Stephanie the entire afternoon so I could get some sleep in the waiting room. She also brought me bags of ribbon she'd found at a craft store that was going out of business. I did a lot of crafts, and she knew I would be thrilled, which I was. She walked into the hospital carrying three huge bags of ribbon and handed them to me. That was the sweetest thing anyone has ever done for me.

I miss my Aunt Jean. She passed away a few months ago, and I hope she continues to watch over me. She was a wonderful person, quite the opposite of her sister. She always told me she loved me every time we talked, and I never ever got that from my mother. There were a valued few wonderful women in my family who tried to make up for the love I lacked with my mother, like my grandmother until I was six and my father's Aunt Lillian after grandma died. Unfortunately, she lived in Hanford, California, so I didn't get to spend time with her very often.

These women helped mold me in a positive way, and then that blessing was passed on to my child. They showed me an example of what a good, loving parent looked like, and I always patterned myself after these fine women.

❧ 10 ❧

Living in Dallas, Oregon, was one of the hardest times in my life. Life was extremely stressful there, and I experienced most of my abuse from my husband in this town. We had been living in a nice townhouse in Salem, but Steve was from Dallas. His entire family lived there, and he was dying to get back to this little bedroom town. I finally gave in.

Stephanie was about six months old at the time. I loved showing her off. We needed some groceries, so I put Stephanie in her stroller and we walked to the grocery store. That way I could show her off to everyone we passed on the way.

I was verbally and almost physically attacked by one of my mother-in-law's friends they called "Fat Pat." She came up to me screaming at the top of her lungs and acted like she was going to hit me. She didn't care that I had my baby with me. I had to be escorted out of the store by an employee. It was awful. She attacked me over the car accident with Kathy and the drama with the insurance company. I was so hated in this town that nobody would have anything to do with me because of this.

If I had it to do over again, I think I would have just signed the release form. I wasn't trying to get rich off the accident, but I needed my medical bills paid. They were all afraid that I would tell the truth. They were afraid I would say that Kathy was in fact drinking that night. She had lied to me about drinking alcohol and then lied to everyone else except her parents that she was too drunk to drive. Kathy had been drinking straight vodka out of a water glass to hide the fact from me that she had been drinking all night. I was threatened by them all and so scared I never told a soul she was drinking. I remember being threatened one night by her father in his old beat-up pickup. He told me I had better not tell anyone during the insurance deposition— or else. I never told anyone, not even my lawyer. I was truly scared of these people and the entire town for that matter. Living there was pure hell.

Don't anyone concern yourself with the fact that I am still fighting a brain injury from the accident and could have died. Let's just focus on poor little Kathy's reputation instead.

Talk about mob mentality. Welcome to Dallas.

I never told my parents about being abused because I was so embarrassed. My saving grace was my sweet girl and my neighbor, Stooge. Her real name was Evelyn, but everyone called her "Stooge." I never knew the story behind the name, but it just seemed to fit her. She was a tough old bird and I loved her. She was so good to me and Stephanie, and I knew if we ever needed anything she would be there for us. She was a good friend to me when I really needed one.

Stooge was a very interesting lady, too. She used to be a bartender in a pretty hardcore biker bar in Dallas, and prior to that she lost her middle finger in a mill accident. She had such a colorful past and told the best stories. She always told me she loved me like the daughter she never had.

When I finally left Dallas, I never looked back, which means I never saw my friend Stooge again. I couldn't bring myself to go back to that town until at least twenty years later. By that time, Stooge had passed away.

The house we rented in Dallas was a nightmare of a dump: linoleum floors, no carpet anywhere, and very tiny. Wood floors and wood paneling in Stephanie's nursery. Carpenter ants everywhere and lights that exploded in the kitchen and pantry. I went to my landlord with my concerns, but he clearly didn't want to be bothered by me. He finally had his "friend," the fire chief, come inspect. He said everything was normal. *Normal? It's normal for light bulbs to explode?* Anyone could have seen it was a fire hazard. I had to finally go get documentation from another realtor I knew in town to threaten my landlord into getting an exterminator out there to get rid of the ants.

I can't even count the amount of times he gave us eviction notices. Every time I needed him for something or had another complaint, some stranger would post an eviction notice on our front door, and not because we didn't pay our rent. I was just too much of a pain, I guess. The house was finally put up for sale, and I knew, now, this was going to be my time to finally make my grand escape.

Steve's drinking had become more and more intense. Every spare moment he had was spent drinking. I was constantly cleaning up stinky beer cans. He also chewed tobacco. The beer cans usually had tobacco spit in them, and I was the one who always cleaned them out. Despite the abuse and neglect, I was still trying to please him.

I had a birthday party for him once at his favorite dive bar in Dallas. That night I was sitting next to him at a long table full of all his drunk friends. I reached out to get a drink of my beer and accidentally grabbed his old beer bottle full of tobacco spit and took a drink. I can't even begin to describe how gross that was. If I ever could make him happy, it wasn't long-lasting. The demons came out with the booze. He was a really nice, good-looking guy until he started drinking. It's like everything changed. Just add alcohol.

One night, we invited a married couple we were friends with to come over. They were hanging out, and I was doing a craft project, stenciling pictures on the floor, and the wife was helping me with it. All of a sudden, for no apparent reason, Steve blurts out to me, "What did you do, write the book dumb like me?" What I should have said was, "No, Steve, but many years from now I'm going to write a book about what an abusive ass you are."

I was so floored and so embarrassed and, for once, I was speech-less. The other guy there stood up for me and said, "What the hell is your problem Steve?" and shut him up. The thing I learned that night is this: abusive men will usually cower to other men in the room. If I could only have another man around guarding me all the time. His abuse was both physical as well as verbal. He would say things to me like, "For fifty cents I'd smash your face in." *Just what every woman wants to hear.* He strangled me frequently to near unconsciousness. One time, he picked me up by my neck and threw me against the front window. Luckily, I didn't go through it, but he wouldn't have cared. Usually he picked me up by my neck and threw me either directly on the floor, or, when he was feeling nice, he threw me on the couch. I always had bruises, mainly on my neck and arms, sometimes on my face. I went through a lot of makeup trying to cover it all up.

He always got a certain look in his eyes, and I knew I had better back off and shut up or I was going to get hurt. It's hard to understand how he would get these blind rages. It's also hard to understand that we never really argued that much. It was just when he got drunk he would black out and rage uncontrollably. The intensity of this was not wasted on me. I learned quickly how much danger I could be in and that I needed to tread lightly. These were terrifying moments, and I didn't know whom I was married to anymore. I'm surprised he didn't get into more bar fights. I think it's because part of him was afraid of what other men could do to him. He always came home from hanging out at the bar without his wedding ring on. I needed to find a way to escape this man or else someday he will go too far and I will end up dead.

Another time he got angry I had flushed his marijuana down the toilet. I was fed up with dealing with what this drug was doing to him. I grabbed Stephanie out of her bassinet, ran upstairs with her, and closed ourselves off in the bedroom. I even placed a box of heavy books in front of the door so he couldn't get to us. I was terrified of him and afraid Stephanie would need a bottle soon, which unfortunately was downstairs in the kitchen. I would be in real danger if I left the bedroom now. I remember thinking, *Please don't cry, baby. Please don't cry.*

He was outside the door. pounding on it and yelling and cursing at me like a wild animal. He was threatening to kill me as soon as he could get to me. I had never seen him like that before. He was out of his mind with anger. This felt like a really bad dream, but I was awake with only a box of books to save me from him. This was the first time I felt like I needed to save me and my baby. He was a monster out there in the hallway. I certainly didn't know him anymore. *Thank God I used to read a lot*, I remember thinking. That box of books was really heavy and saved me and my precious girl from him. We had a phone in the bedroom, but instead of calling 911, I called his parents to come over and help me out. I made a big mistake by calling them. His father was a man of few to no words, and all he said was, "Steve, don't hit your wife."

Oh great. Thanks, Bob. That really helped.

The second they left, Steve was even more enraged and came after me again. My daughter and I waited up in the bedroom for hours for him to pass out on the couch downstairs. I waited for what seemed like forever, then finally everything was quiet. I carefully opened the door and walked down the stairs. Finally, he was asleep on the couch. Now is my chance to get out, so I called my father to come and get us. By this time, it was around five in the morning. I packed all of our things, and we carried everything out of the house right in front of Steve. He never woke up. The couch he passed out on was right exactly next to the front door and, luckily, he never once woke up.

I have a serious problem. I spent about three weeks with my parents debating what to do. Steve was very apologetic *for the umpteenth time* and promised it would never, ever happen again. Yet, in that moment, I felt a little sorry for him and really hated being at my parents' house, so I went back. *Maybe things will get better now.*

It took me all afternoon to clean up all the beer cans that were scattered throughout the house. Despite the history of abuse that intensified as soon as I announced I was pregnant, I blamed myself— all the extra stress of having a wife and a new baby. Also, the fact that our baby had almost died at such a young and vulnerable age added to the stress. However, I was under all this stress, too, and I didn't turn to alcohol or drugs.

I always had a deep sense of love and responsibility where Stephanie was concerned. I knew all her different cries and what she needed at different times throughout the day. I loved being her mommy, and I was never going to let her down. I guess you could say it was an overwhelming need to make sure she was OK and that all her needs were met. This was about my sweet girl now, not me. She was an innocent and helpless little girl, and she would need me to always be there to make sure she was safe, healthy, and happy. However, that means I take care of her mommy too. *I need to find a way to escape this man or else someday he will go too far and I will end up dead.* This thought went through my mind so many times before I finally took action.

I got a job in Dallas working at a bank. Luckily, I found a very sweet grandma to babysit Stephanie while I was at work. I had to work full-time. We were desperate for money. I wished so much I could stay home with Stephanie, but that was impossible. I have so much empathy for moms who have to leave their babies and go to work. It's very hard, especially when your child cries every morning when you leave.

It never failed. Stephanie would start to cry as I was leaving, and then I would cry all the way to work. When I arrived at work, I called the babysitter to check on her and she was always fine. I had to pack so much every day to take to the babysitter's, too. I packed her high chair, playpen, car seat, and stroller, along with the usual diaper bag and food. I packed everything back up to take home after work, then started all over again the next day. The life of a working mother. I adored Martha, our babysitter. She was so good to my girl, and Stephanie adored her too. I should have never told my mother where Martha lived or how to contact her.

We were so poor, and it was all I could do to pay the rent and keep the electricity turned on. I remember being so excited when I found out we were going to get $350 back from our taxes. This was substantial money to me, and it would really help with our bills and food. Unfortunately, Steve got to the mailbox before I did the day it arrived. He forged my signature, cashed the check, took it straight to the nearest sporting goods store, and spent the entire thing on hunting and fishing gear. I was fuming. I should have reported him for forgery. I never once called the police on him, and there were hundreds of times I should have. I always knew eventually he would get out and then there would be hell to pay. I was in preservation mode, not just for myself, but for my daughter, too.

I decided I needed to get a second job. Martha agreed to watch Stephanie some nights, too. I got a part-time job at a restaurant/bar next door to the bank I worked at. I didn't want to be away from Stephanie that long, but times were desperate.

One day, Stephanie got an ear infection. I didn't dare ask for more time off because I was already on probation for being absent and late to work too many times. Luckily, Martha offered to take Stephanie to her doctor for me. I was supposed to start my first night at the restaurant job that same night. Unfortunately, Martha had other plans and couldn't watch her. So, I called my mother and asked her if she could watch Stephanie for a couple of hours. She agreed and went to Martha's to pick her up. Mom found out that Martha had taken Stephanie to the doctor instead of me. She was outraged because I didn't take time off work to take Stephanie to the doctor myself. I guess that made me the worst mother on the planet.

Mom was so angry at me she drove over to the restaurant to tell me off. I was in the parking lot, about to walk into my new job for the first time, when she pulled up. Mom screeched her new Cadillac to a stop and jumped out. She freaked out in the middle of the parking lot with my daughter in the back seat of her car. She screamed at me about what a horrible and neglectful mother I was and refused to even let me say hi to Stephanie. That was the closest I have ever come to hitting my mother. The last thing she said to me was that she was going to get legal custody of my daughter because I was an unfit mother. Then she got in the car, closed the door in my face, and took off.

Here I go again. Now what do I do? Well, screw the new job. I have to go rescue my daughter from the psychotic lady holding her prisoner in her car.

I got in my car and chased her all the way home. They lived in Salem, which is about a half hour away from Dallas. She refused to pull over and refused to even look at me. I wasn't going to do anything that would cause Crazy to crash her car with my child in it, so I kept my distance the entire way to her house. Mom was constantly threatening me with taking away my baby and having me deemed unfit. One time, I asked to borrow twenty dollars from them to purchase cereal. Well, I'm unfit and she needs to legally take my baby from me. I lived in constant fear that she was going to try to take me to court and take my baby away from me. Instead of supporting me as a new mother, she criticized everything I did and tried to make me feel like I wasn't capable of being a mother. My mother was a monster. She also had everyone in the family fooled into believing she was raising my daughter in place of me.

We all arrived at my mother's house, and Dad didn't have a clue what was going on. I wasn't about to have a screaming match with my mother in front of my daughter, so I carefully managed to wrangle Stephanie away from her and we got the hell out of there. I wasn't about to stay and risk being held hostage again while she yells at me about what a loser mother I am, especially not in front of my daughter. Dad would easily join in with her, too. He wasn't going to risk her rage turning on him. He was used to sacrificing his kids. I was out of there forever. *How dare she take my daughter like this.* Stephanie was never going to experience a scene like that ever again. It was one thing for me to have endured it many times over, but not my precious girl.

It took six months before I broke my vow and allowed my mother around us again. My mother's biggest ace in the hole was my father. He was a master at calming situations and bringing people back together. He was so good at it because he'd had so much practice. He was constantly mediating between mom, and, well, everyone.

I lost the job I never started at the restaurant. I would have to figure something else out. *But for now, just breathe.* One evening, Martha called me almost too angry to speak. My mother had called her and accused her son of molesting my daughter. I couldn't believe what I was hearing. It was completely ridiculous. Her son was rarely even there, and how did my mother even know she had a son?

I did my best to calm Martha down, but the damage had already been done. Martha politely but firmly quit as my babysitter. It broke my heart, not just because she wouldn't watch Stephanie anymore but also because my mother had caused her so much stress. I also think the most disgusting, deplorable thing you can do to another person is to accuse them of molesting a child when it isn't true. I hated that she tried to do this to Martha's son. It is pure evil to accuse an innocent person of doing this for your own revenge.

Pure evil.

❦ 11 ❧

Are you wondering why I would ever allow my mother to spend a second with my child? This is a tough one because I desperately wanted my child to have grandparents. I wasn't allowed this privilege after the age of six, and I feel they are important to have in a child's life, that is, if they are stable.

Before Stephanie was born, I had a talk with both parents. I told them if they wanted to spend time with their grandchild, Mom would have to get some help first and get on some medication, if that was necessary, or I wasn't going to be leaving my child in their care. To my surprise, she actually went and got evaluated. The specialist diagnosed her with "severe depression disorder" and prescribed Prozac. This medication really seemed to help her a lot, and it was a relief to me. She frequently went off the medication, but, fortunately for me, I had the ability to know instantly when she went off it.

I never allowed her to be alone with Stephanie during those times. I wasn't trying to punish her. I was looking out for my daughter. I also told her if she ever freaked out in front of Stephanie even once, that would be the end. I would never allow my daughter to experience a second of what my brother and I had to endure. Stephanie had a really good relationship with her grandparents, I am proud to say. I wanted a different experience for her than I'd had, and I accomplished this by getting my mother the help she needed. I didn't feel it was fair for me to keep Stephanie away from having grandparents because I had a bad relationship with my mom. Unfortunately, it wasn't enough in the long run, but it gave us a few good years.

I thought it was important to encourage a relationship with her grandparents as long as it could last. I wasn't given the ability to have any grandparents after my Grandma Eva died, and it wasn't because my other set of grandparents were dead either. My mother hated her parents. They were both very much alive and lived only about ten minutes from our house. It was because, for some reason, Mom didn't like them and wouldn't allow us to be around them, ever. This isn't really that surprising, is it? You are beginning to realize my mother is a bit off, right?

To this day, I never really knew the true reason why they were such horrible people. I wonder what it must have felt like to them to live so close to their grandchildren and never get to see them. I have been told many different reasons over the years. The one I was told the most was that they hated my father because he was Catholic. Years later, I found out they lived across the street from my Catholic grade school and right next door to the priest. So, this doesn't make any sense. If they truly hated Catholics, then why would they live across the street from a Catholic church and grade school? The saddest part is, our playground was in the school parking lot right in front of their house. I often wondered if they ever watched us play outside during our recess. Makes me feel so sad that this is probably the only time they ever saw us when we were little, or, did they even know it was us they were looking at?

It was also so strange at Christmas when our cousins would ask us, very innocently, what gifts we'd gotten from Grandma and Grandpa. Our answer was always, "Nothing." Of course, they always got some really nice presents from them. Our cousins raved about our grandparents and they loved them a lot. All of my cousins were allowed to spend time with them.

My grandparents' names were Buck and Clarice. Buck was his nickname. His real name was Walter. Clarice was really little, only about four-foot-nine-inches tall, but boy was she a tough, little lady. We were also told that Buck was abusive to Mom, but my aunt says she never once witnessed that. Her brother echoes the same sentiment that nothing ever happened. Years after Buck's death, Mom accused him of sexually abusing her when she was two years old. I don't know if any of that's true or not, but why did she wait so long to tell that story? It isn't my place to comment; however, I don't agree with accusing people of things when they aren't there to defend themselves.

It wasn't until I was sixteen when I was able to finally get to know my grandparents. I really did yearn for the love of grandparents. I felt cheated out of having grandparents. Up to that point, I'd never had a grandfather. My father's father died before I was born. My Grandma Eva remarried, but he wasn't a very nice person and wanted nothing to do with us kids. He even made us purchase items my grandma made in his garage sale after grandma died. These things had sentimental value only to us, but he still felt we should pay him to get to keep them. *Stand-up guy, right?* My uncle lived at home while he attended Willamette Law school, and word on the street was that he hated this guy. I never saw him after that garage sale. One day, I heard he had died and left all his money to the Catholic church. I heard he was very wealthy too. A lot of people were upset that he didn't think of the family, but I didn't care. I don't feel I deserved any of his money because I didn't have any kind of relationship with him.

I heard that Buck, my mother's father, was in the hospital and wasn't expected to make it. I learned this because I was eavesdropping on a conversation between my mother and my aunt. I wasn't aware of what his illness was, but I decided I wanted to pay him a visit. Because I had a driver's license, I was able to drive myself secretly to the hospital to see him. I didn't dare let my mother know I was going. She would have thrown another one of her fits. I wonder if any other kids had to sneak around to see their grandparents.

I nervously drove to the hospital and asked the front desk what room he was in. I stood there in the doorway of his room for what felt like a really long time, too afraid to walk in. I wasn't sure if he were still alive either. He laid there so still.

All of a sudden, I heard a very deep voice say, "I hear you're my granddaughter."

I paused for a moment, almost wanting to run away, but then I said, "I hear you're my grandfather."

That was the beginning of our relationship. Sounds strange, doesn't it? However, it helped to break the ice, and I was then able to walk into the room and stand next to him. We had some meaningless chitchat, and I never asked him what was wrong with him or why he was in the hospital. I probably didn't feel comfortable enough to ask, or I didn't think it was any of my business.

Finally, he said to me, "If I make it, will you come see me?"

"Yes, I will," I answered.

"But don't expect me to be a granddaughter to you now that I'm a grown-up when you weren't a grandfather to me when I was a little girl."

We made a deal, and by some miracle he survived. I still had to sneak over to their house to see them. I kept my word and went to visit them, all the while never disclosing to any of my family that I was seeing them. I finally told my Aunt Jean because I trusted her to keep my secret. She was going to go over to their house to make them Thanksgiving dinner, and I wanted to come hang out and help her with it.

We were really starting to get to know each other when I found out my Grandma Clarice had already been diagnosed with Alzheimer's disease. Unfortunately, she progressed fast. It ended our getting to know each other before it really even had a chance. Eventually she was placed in a nursing home. She always called me "Shirley." I went to see her every day after work and brought her little presents. Every time when I was leaving, she would say, "Nice to meet you, Shirley." I would always say, "Nice to meet you too, Grandma."

She especially liked the sweatshirts I brought her. That was her favorite thing, and she loved to put her bra on the outside of the sweatshirt and I would say, "Grandma, that goes on the inside," and she would laugh. It should have been devastating that she had this illness, but it really wasn't so bad. Even though she told me it was nice to meet me every single day, I still enjoyed my visits with her. She could tell me things that happened fifty years ago but not what happened fifty minutes ago. She was so feisty, too.

Buck had to eventually be placed in the same nursing home, but Clarice didn't want to share a room with him. She had already gotten herself a little boyfriend in the nursing home. She used to lock herself in her boyfriend's room, and when the nurses tried to get her out, she attacked them with his haircomb. She also escaped quite frequently, which is still a mystery to me how in the world she managed that. The fence was at least eight feet tall and she was half that size. She climbed the fence in her slippers, carried her blanket with her, and walked up the street. I am not sure what she needed the blanket for, but every time she escaped she was wearing her slippers and carrying the same blanket.

We frequently got called from the nursing home that Clarice had escaped again, and I knew exactly where to go to find her. We would go pick her up and take her back, which broke my heart every time. There was a reason she kept escaping, I'm sure, but I certainly wasn't equipped to take care of her. It wasn't so tragic though. For the most part, she seemed really happy. I loved to listen to her laugh. She had the sweetest voice and the cutest giggle. I wish I had known her before her illness, but I made the best of it. At least I finally had the chance to get to know them, even if it was for a short period of time.

⚜ 12 ⚜

My boss at the bank was worried about me. She called me into the conference room to have a chat. This always made me nervous because I was so paranoid about losing my job. She was noticing bruises all over my neck and wanted to talk to me about it. She had noticed other bruising in the past, but I just made up some lie about where it came from. This time I didn't lie. Instead, I broke down and cried.

I told her everything, poured my heart out to her that day. She listened to me and said I should call the police next time, or maybe get out. I had already been planning my escape for the last few months. I knew I had to be very sneaky and careful if I were going to make it out alive. This could affect my sweet girl too. I needed to get out as soon as possible, but I didn't want to put either one of us in any danger. I didn't want Stephanie to grow up to believe this was normal either. I was terrified she would grow up and marry the same kind of person, and that destroyed me more than anything Steve could have ever done to me.

However, he said he would kill me if I ever left, and I completely believed him. I appreciated everything my boss said to me, but I still had to keep my plan quiet. Plus, I wanted my boss to believe I still had my shit together. *I am planning on getting the hell out of here, but for now I still need my job.* I trusted nobody in that town and, unfortunately, that included my boss. I believe now she just wanted to be my friend, but I had to keep my eye on the prize and that was saving myself and, more importantly, my Stephanie.

I was always so ashamed and embarrassed. Always hiding bruises. I know now this wasn't my fault, but, somehow, each time he beat me up, he blamed me. He would say things like, "If you hadn't made me so mad," or, "You know better than to keep yappin' when I am getting angry."

Seriously, you are the one with the problem jackass, not me. How dare you treat me like this.

Each time I took a beating from him could have been the end of me. He went into what I used to call a "blind rage" and acted like he didn't remember what he did to me. Maybe there really is such a thing, and that is terrifying. I used to think, *When he finally kills me, his defense will be accidental death caused by blind rage.* He was also cheating on me left and right. I started sleeping on the couch every night he was home. I wasn't going to take a chance on getting some disease from him. He would regularly get drunk at the local dive bar then bring his skanky friends home at three in the morning, wake me up, and demand I make them all burgers.

Are you kidding me? You just woke up the baby, jerk. Fix it yourself. I need to take care of my daughter. Oh, by the way, get off my planet and take your skanky friends with you.

I started hiding money in the freezer. I knew we lived in a fire hazard, and, if the place did catch fire, at least the money would be safe, hopefully. I felt like a gangster skimming money from a casino. I was skimming as much as I could off each paycheck and hiding it all in the freezer. It was the most intense year of my entire life. My plan for escape is what kept me going. It seemed like everything came together perfectly, all at the same time, when it was time for me to leave. First, my car accident settlement came through. I think I got around $3,000. I desperately needed that. The dump we lived in finally had a buyer, so we had to move. All this happened within the span of one week. It was time for me to put my plan into motion.

I convinced Steve that we needed to separate. I never mentioned the word "divorce" to him because I knew that would be too dangerous. I suggested we needed a break from one another, a little time apart. He agreed with me and didn't attempt to threaten my life this time. I went to a used car lot and purchased a land yacht of a car for $500. I needed a car. I had already sold my cute, little 280z for money to live on. It was so ugly, and the doors squeaked when you opened them, but it ran. My only criteria at the time for a car was dependability. It was a far cry from the cute little 280z I used to own, but times were desperate now.

Now I need to find a job in Salem because, when I do finally move, I am getting the hell out of Dallas. I managed to find time each day to hunt for a job. I had already developed a plan and an angle for a job. When Stephanie was three weeks old and spent five days in an isolation room at the hospital, we were a week away from having medical coverage. There was a month waiting period back in those days. We owed the hospital a little over $15,000.

My plan was for them to give me a job and then they could take a percentage of my paycheck to start paying them back. I told them they didn't stand a chance getting paid if they counted on her father. I was praying this would work. I went there every single day for two weeks and, finally, they had an opening. I was hired as an admitting clerk in the emergency room. They took a percentage out each pay period, and I managed to get them paid off, eventually. However, one day I got a check in the mail from the hospital. They had decided to stop taking a percentage of my wages and sent me to collection. It wasn't like I had stopped paying them. They were authorized to take it out of my paycheck. I couldn't believe it.

Then the collection calls started coming in. These people were brutal. I couldn't believe the disgusting things they were calling me. I remember saying to them, "You get that these were all medical bills, right?" They didn't care. It made no difference to them. Their only job was to bully as much money out of me as they could and as quickly as they could. The hospital never gave me a reason for sending me to collections either. I could have just ignored everyone and not paid them back, but my pride and my morals wouldn't allow it. I was grateful to the nurses and doctors that helped my daughter, but the bureaucracy of the hospital—not so much.

I was so good at convincing Steve we needed to separate now that the house was sold, he even helped me move into my new apartment in Salem. No way in hell was I staying in Dallas. It was so incredibly refreshing and freeing to get out. He stayed in Dallas. To keep everything cordial, I helped him move into his new apartment, too. *Maybe now that we are apart we can be good parents to Stephanie and things will get better.* I convinced him we just needed to separate, but the truth was I had already made an appointment to see a divorce attorney the following Monday. I wasn't wasting any time.

I sued for divorce and full custody of Stephanie. Steve was served the divorce papers the following week, and to say he was mad would be an understatement. I had tricked him and now he knew the truth. He drove over to my new apartment in Salem and almost busted down my door. I really didn't realize exactly how much danger I was in at the time, but fortunately for me I was thinking quickly on my feet. He came into my apartment and literally picked me up and held me upside down.

Without warning, he dropped me on my head.

He made a fist and was about to hit me when I said, "Go ahead. All I have to do is scream and the two big guys that live upstairs will come running."

He made some vulgar gesture at me and then he left.

I couldn't believe it worked. I'd completely made that whole thing up. I had no idea who lived in the apartment upstairs or if anyone at all even lived there. There weren't two big guys living upstairs. What I learned from this is that men who hit women are afraid of other men.

Big, tough guy . . . You can hit a woman, but you turn and run at the threat of another man? Interesting.

Stephanie was only a year old and wouldn't remember the abuse and hopefully wouldn't be affected negatively by any of this. I was awarded full custody of Stephanie, and that was really all I cared about. He was ordered to pay me $250 a month in child support, but I knew I would never see it. I finally applied for a court order to have him garnished for the child support I was still waiting to get a year later.

What did he do when he got word of the garnishment? Quit his job. I was still allowing him to have his weekly visits. I believed the two issues should be separate. It would take some time, but eventually the courts would catch up to where he was working and order another garnishment.

This time his mommy hired an attorney to get his child support lowered. *Lowered to what?* I remember thinking. He wasn't paying me anything. Well, it worked, and the judge lowered his support order to $103 a month instead of $250. I couldn't believe it, but, honestly, I really didn't care.

Stephanie was and always has been my responsibility. I often wondered how they felt about what they did, but I wasn't going to let it affect me. I mean, in the end they "won," but did they feel guilty that they basically took that money away from their own granddaughter? I think they always figured they were just sticking it to me, but who were they really hurting with this? I didn't let it get to me. I was too happy because I was finally away from him, except for when he came to pick Stephanie up.

My attorney, on the other hand, was very upset, and it was pretty enjoyable watching him read Steve the riot act that day. He told him he was the most worthless piece of crap he had ever met. He said, "I hope you are proud you just shit on your own kid." I didn't see it that way, but my attorney was right. Why didn't he care that she was well-cared for and that I had enough money to buy her clothing and food and give her the best things in life I possibly could?

Well, that was *my* job and *my* responsibility, and I never once looked to him or anyone else for these things. I didn't before we were divorced, and I never did after.

13

eeping Stephanie safe, however, proved to be more work than
I could have ever imagined. We were divorced, and I had sole
custody of Stephanie, but Steve still had his rights to every-
other-weekend visits and one day during the week. I don't recall him
ever using his Wednesday night visits with her, but he always took her
every other weekend. I always worried when he took her, but nothing
like this one Friday night. He came and picked her up and headed back
to Dallas, as usual. As the night went on, however, I kept getting this
nagging feeling that something was wrong.

So, at around 10:00 pm I called him to check on her. There was no
answer. That wasn't completely out of the ordinary. He enjoyed playing
games with me. I tried again an hour later—still no answer. A sense of
dread came over me. I got to the point where I couldn't take it
anymore so I got in my car and drove the half hour to his apartment in
Dallas.

I arrived at his apartment, knocked on the door, and waited. There
was no answer. I reached for the door handle. It turned easily, so I
walked in. I couldn't believe what I saw. There on the floor, in the
middle of the room, was my precious girl sound asleep. *Asleep on the
dirty floor wearing just a diaper in the middle of winter.*

Why wasn't she in her crib? Where is her father? Well, he was passed out on the couch, of course. How many times did I tell him not to drink when he had Stephanie? I was beside myself with anger, and my first inclination was to punch him as hard as I could in the face and yell at him. However, there was still that other issue of him being a vicious drunk. I managed to get her dressed and her and all her things out the front door, and he never woke up. Maybe I should have waked him up to tell him I was taking her with me, but, honestly, I really didn't care. I just wanted to get out of there. I also hoped to put some fear into him so he would straighten his act up and be a responsible father.

Ironically, I was threatened by his attorney with contempt of court and told that I would be arrested if I ever pulled anything like that again. *Hell yes, I would do it again.* There is not one single thing I wouldn't do for my daughter, especially if it put her safety at risk. Next time, however, maybe I should call the police first. Luckily, this never happened again, but, unfortunately, plenty of other bad things happened instead.

Another behavior of his that drove me nuts was that he made plans to take Stephanie places then would cancel the day of. One particular time, he told her he had bought them tickets to go to the circus. Stephanie was so excited all week to go to the circus. The day of the circus came and, again, he called and cancelled. Luckily, I was able to get a few tickets so my parents could take her because I had to work that day. I finally had to stop telling Stephanie when he was planning to take her somewhere because most of the time he cancelled. The rare times he didn't cancel, well, those would just become nice surprises for her. I wasn't going to allow her to be continually disappointed, so I did what I had to do to protect her.

It amazes me how much crap a biological parent can pull and still have legal rights to their child. For example, Steve had a girlfriend named June who liked to party as much as, or maybe even more than, he did. What a toxic duo they turned out to be. One weekend after her visit to her dad's, Stephanie came home and told me that Steve and June had tied her down to her bed so they could go out to the bar. Was I hearing this right?

What did you just say, Sweetie? Wait a minute, what? *Your father tied you down to your bed and then left you there? Alone? Left the house? How long were they gone? Were you scared?* I am going to kill him.

I couldn't believe he had done this to her. She must have been so scared. How could he do this to her? He should lose any rights he has to his child forever for doing this, right? Wrong. Shocking, isn't it? I was beyond livid. I mean, did he consider the amount of danger he was putting his child in so he could go out and get drunk? What if the house caught fire? What would she do? What if she had to use the bathroom? What if she heard a noise or someone tried to break in? *What if . . . What the hell if?* There are too many what-ifs. How terrifying that must have been for her to be tied to the bed and left all alone.

I am feeling my blood boil just thinking about it. This happened a long time ago and it still feels fresh and painful. How dare he do this to her. He didn't lose his rights. I still had to let her go with him every other weekend. I decided to appeal to his parents. I knew they loved Stephanie, and I knew they wouldn't want her to be put in any danger, so I called his mother and completely ratted him out to her. I told her everything that was going on.

After that, when it was his weekend, Steve picked Stephanie up and dropped her off at his parents' house where she stayed the entire weekend. *Thank God it worked.* At least now I could have some peace of mind knowing that the grandparents would be watching over her. I was thankful that I had a better relationship with his parents since we had divorced. I could communicate with his mother and at least know that Stephanie was in safer hands. In his family, Mama ruled the roost. She was a very strong personality, and he was easily controlled by her. He continued to drop Stephanie off at his parents every weekend he had her, until this one dreadful week.

Stephanie was six, and Steve had his usual weekend visit. He always picked her up Friday night at 6:00 p.m. and brought her home Sunday night at 6:00 p.m. Well, Sunday night comes around and it's after 6:00 p.m. and no Stephanie. The phone rings and it's Steve. I figured he was going to tell me they were just running late and they would be here soon. Nope, that wasn't what he was calling to say. Instead, he said that he was keeping her and I was never going to see her again.

Wait, what? Seriously? Stop! What are you doing? and then *click*—he hung up on me.

My body slowly sunk to the floor and I was hysterical with fear. *Is this really happening?* It felt like my worst nightmare just came true. I quickly pulled myself together and called my lawyer. His adorable little girl answered the phone and told me her daddy was up in a tree. I said, "Well, this is a very important emergency. Can you please go get daddy and have him call me?" It would have been more adorable if I hadn't been in such a state of sheer panic. Bless her heart, she wrote down my phone number and within minutes my lawyer called me back.

My lawyer instructed me to come to his office in the morning so we could discuss how I was going to get my daughter back. I didn't sleep at all that night. I was so panicked that I might not ever see my girl again. Where on earth could she be? He told me I was never going to see her again. *What is wrong with you*, I thought. *How dare you do this, not just to me, but to Stephanie.* All I hoped was that she was OK and wasn't scared.

I rushed to my lawyer the next day. The only recourse he offered was to send a threatening letter to my ex's lawyer to persuade Steve to bring her back. The courts didn't worry too much if they knew the child was in the hands of a biological parent, no matter what the circumstances. This felt like such a nightmare to me. We had no idea where they were. He could have taken her to another country by now for all I knew, but we are just going to wait and see what happens? I didn't think I could take this. I have seen shows before where the parent took the child to another country and they were never seen again. I was nearly hysterical with fear. This is going to be the thing that sends me over the edge, but no, I need to be strong for my girl. I can't allow him to have all this power and control over me. When this is over, I am going to take measures to keep him permanently out of our lives.

It ended up taking me a week to get her back. It was the longest week of my life. Steve called me every day to badger me and remind me that his intention was for me to never see her again. *What a bully.* That's what he was doing: bullying me and enjoying it when I cried and begged for him to let me speak to Stephanie. He didn't care about our little contempt of court threat, and because he was her father, he had rights, and nobody got very excited about doing anything other than myself. I was a wreck. I pleaded and begged him to bring Stephanie home. I could hear Stephanie in the background crying and asking to talk to Mommy. Jerk never once let me talk to her. He was tormenting us both, and the thought of him upsetting her was more than I could take. This was total domination and control over me, and he enjoyed every minute of it. *Sick bastard.*

One afternoon when he called me, I was finally able to record his threatening phone call. I quickly hit the "record" button and recorded the entire disturbing phone call. I could also hear Stephanie crying in the background. Still, he wouldn't let me to talk to her. I believed his intention was mental torment and control over me, but did he once consider what this could be doing to his daughter? I took this recording right to my attorney's office. I didn't even have an appointment, but I knew this was a turning point in getting her home, and I was right. My attorney was so disgusted at what he heard on that tape he went into action and I got her back the very next day. It turned out that he was keeping Stephanie at his girlfriend June's sister's house in a small town outside of Dallas called Falls City.

I was able to get her back on a Friday afternoon. The transfer took place at his parents' house. I didn't even see him. However, that very weekend was his weekend to have her, and guess what the court made me do? I had to allow her to go spend the weekend with her father. After the nightmare he just put me and Stephanie through. I had to willingly turn her back over to him. They said I could go to jail if I didn't let her go. *Screwy system.* There is so much wrong with all of this. I didn't have a choice. I had to let her go.

I was so relieved when I found out she'd stayed at his parent's house all weekend. Although I had called them numerous times when Stephanie was missing, they would never tell me where she was. I know they knew exactly where she was the whole time. *Oh yes, they knew.* They had to have known. I seriously considered getting us both visas and moving to another country. Just take my girl and go hide out somewhere. I never trusted she was at all safe in his care, and he continually did things to reinforce this.

The thing that kept me from actually acting on it though was Stephanie. I didn't know how she would feel years from now being taken away from her family. I couldn't bear the thought of her being angry at me. The truth is, Steve wanted to drive me crazy and torture me more than he wanted to be a father. He was all about dominance and control, but not so good at parenting.

He would probably never agree with this, but I desperately wanted Steve to be a good father. I wanted him to spend time with Stephanie as long as he wasn't endangering her, of course. Stephanie deserved to have good, responsible parents on her side. She needed and deserved for us both to have her back, to always put her first. *Grow the hell up, asshole.* I went many times to talk to drug and alcohol counselors to get him some help. He refused to ever go. His own mother even went with me a few times. I did this for Stephanie. She deserved so much more than she got from him. He missed out on a wonderful girl too.

He took her regularly until she was about seven or eight, then the visits became fewer and fewer until one day they just stopped. When Stephanie graduated from high school, we invited him to her graduation and to the party we had at our house afterward. I was shocked when he came up to me and thanked me personally for doing such a good job raising Stephanie. He then went outside where Jeff, my husband, was barbecuing and thanked him for being a good father to her as well.

I would imagine he has quite a few regrets. I don't hold any animosity toward him today. I wish him well, and I feel bad for him that things turned out this way. He doesn't have a relationship at all with Stephanie. Recently, Stephanie agreed to meet him at a restaurant for dinner. He was a no-show. He was always really good at making the plans but not so good at keeping them.

The sad part is he has a granddaughter now that he has never seen. I couldn't imagine not being there when Eva was born and not getting to spend time every week with her. That would be tragic to me. My father used to say that people create their own problems, and to a great extent I agree. Steve had many, many chances to make things right and never did.

❧ 14 ❧

With all the physical and mental beatings, I developed a real hatred and fear of men. His constant pounding on my head, or picking me up by my neck and throwing me into walls—and once, a window—really took a toll. The constant mental degradation played a part in who I became for quite a while, too. Because of the rape and now this abusive marriage, hating was the easiest and most obvious choice for me to make. The most important lesson I had to learn, however, is that not all people are bad. I know I am not a bad person. I didn't deserve this. For me to move on from all the pain, I had to find a way to forgive. I had to walk through a lot of fire and pain to get to where I could find acceptance and move on.

Another lesson here is, don't settle. Don't marry someone thinking you can fix them or change them. Protect your happiness, but don't block the wall off too high either. Don't miss out on that really good person because you are too blocked off. You don't have to choose to hate or fear anyone or anything. It's a fine line and a really intense journey. Just don't distrust all men or all women. I used to have to remind myself not to paint everyone with the same brush. Abuse throws the abused into this realm of feelings of fear and rage all at the same time.

I'm so enraged at you for doing this to me, yet I'm so terrified you might kill me this time. I replaced love for him with fear of him.

Abuse set the tone for every man I ever dated after that. I deserve a good person in my life and I'm not going to settle. I experienced so much pain, I had to protect my happiness and especially my daughter's, too.

Every day I feel blessed that Stephanie is part of my life. My world is a better place because she is in it and she has made me a better person. She is a remarkable individual and everyone who knows her loves her. Her soul shines the brightest light, and this world is a better place because she is here. I believe she is my miracle, and I know that God kept her here for a reason. She has touched so many lives. My love and pride for her grows every day.

I am in such awe of her mothering skills, too. She is so much more confident and relaxed than I ever was as a new mommy. I remember the first time I heard Eva cry. Stephanie just calmly looked at her and said, "You're OK." I never pushed religion on Stephanie because of my experience growing up Catholic. Even so, Stephanie was a Young Life leader in high school and extremely faithful. Young Life is a Christian fellowship group that mentors middle school through high school girls. I think it meant more to her since it wasn't shoved down her throat and she could come to her faith all on her own. I wish that had been my reality, but I believe my experiences made me who I am and hopefully gave me some wisdom to overcome difficult situations.

I certainly never considered sending her to a Catholic school. With thousands of cases reported of sexual abuse by Catholic staff, how could anyone justify sending their children to a Catholic school? I am glad to hear that things are better in Catholic schools than they used to be. I am not here to slam the Catholic faith, but I definitely will slam the way I and other children of my time were treated. It was barbaric, unspeakable, and definitely cruel. It made me who I am today, and I am finally content with that.

Even though I had many friends I could count on and trust, I always felt subpar to them and most everyone else, too. I had very low self-esteem for a large part of my life. I thought everyone else was better than me. It wasn't until recently I began to learn to love myself.

I have also learned some very valuable lessons along the way about the dangers of speaking negatively about yourself. For me, it was much easier to say something negative about myself than something positive. If I spoke highly of myself, wouldn't that make me look stuck-up? The more you hear something about yourself, the more you will begin to believe it. Whether it's good or bad or if it's not even true, the more you hear it, the more you believe it—especially if it's negative.

For me, negative is so much stronger than positive. That was my experience growing up. I can't count how many times I heard that I was fat, had a big butt, was stupid, annoying, ugly, worthless, and unwanted. Nothing was ever on a positive note, and this stuff became my reality. The more I heard it, the more I believed it. This stuff, *this bullshit,* gets into your psyche and becomes who you are. It writes on the slate of who you become, and it is very difficult to fight through to finally change your belief.

I have learned to try hard to always speak highly of myself no matter how hard and awkward it feels at first. It has gotten easier with time and has made my life more positive. I have learned to believe in myself even when nobody else would. Love yourself. Sometimes you will be all you have. Be willing to give yourself the love you so easily give away to others. You are worth it. Change the tape in your mind to something more positive and good things will follow.

For me to have a more positive life and be a more positive and loving influence to my daughter, I had to start changing the tape of who I was and what I genuinely felt about myself. Change the message in your head from negative to positive and a whole new world of opportunities will open up. Positive thoughts create positive results.

If you don't believe me, what do you have to lose to just give it a try for a while?

✥ 15 ✥

My cousin tried to rape me. I trusted my cousin. Since we were close in age, we always hung out together during our family visits when we were kids. I really adored him, too. I thought we were close and he would always want what's best for me. It was more natural to think he would want to protect me. I was wrong.

He was extremely religious. He wasn't Catholic; he was a born-again Christian, just like his mother. They lived in the Deep South, where religion was king. In 2016, I went on a tour of the old mental hospital in my town. I was reading an old log of diagnoses from the early 1900s and one of them said "religious excitement," which reminded me of my cousin.

He was going through a very rough time back in 2002 after the recent death of his mom. He started to call me a lot after she died and, somehow, I helped him through it. Or, that is what he wanted me to believe. He said he found it comforting talking to me because he was going through such a rough time. He lived in South Carolina.

One day, he called and asked me if he flew out here, would I go with him to this little town in Washington called Leavenworth. It's a town in Washington that is made to look like a town in Germany and is a popular tourist destination. He said he and his wife liked to go there a lot and wondered if I could take a couple days and go there with him. I didn't hesitate. I would do almost anything to help my cousin. He said his wife wouldn't be able to make it. That made my intuition start to alarm me that this wasn't OK, but I ignored it. My husband Jeff trusted him, too.

I picked him up at the Portland airport and we headed to Washington. His plane didn't land until a little after 11:00 p.m., so we found a hotel for the night. My cousin offered to go into the office and get us our rooms. I gave him my credit card to pay for my room and waited. He came back to the car with only one room key. The entire hotel was booked, he told me. We got the last room. That sounded strange to me since it was a Thursday night.

We got in the room, sat down, and he immediately started talking about his feelings for me. He told me he had written me a letter on the plane and wanted to read it to me. I felt awkward, but I kept shaking off the screaming that was now coming from my gut. He pulled out his "letter." However, it was more like a manifesto than just a letter. It was *twelve* pages long. *No way did he write this on the plane*, I remember thinking. This was deliberate premeditation and carefully thought out.

It was the strangest letter I have ever heard. It was full of things like how much I meant to him and how much he has always loved me. It got creepier and creepier as it went on. He wouldn't let me touch "my letter" when I asked to see it. He just kept insisting on reading it to me. It was the first letter I've ever received that I was never going to get my hands on. Later, I realized this was done intentionally, probably so I couldn't keep it as evidence.

After he finished reading his manifesto, he told me he had something he would like me to listen to. He asked me to sit on the bed, lean against the headboard, and close my eyes. I did as he asked while he proceeded to put a headset over my ears. I started feeling afraid. I desperately wanted to trust him, but my intuition was screaming at me to run.

"This is important," he said. "Close your eyes."

Celine Deon's voice engulfed me. He had recorded her love songs to play for me. Before I fully digested what was going on, I felt his weight on me. *He was on top of me, trying to kiss me.* All his 350 pounds of weight was laying on top of me and his lips were on mine. I managed to slide out from underneath him. I hit the ground hard. I couldn't believe what was happening.

Please, God, don't let this be happening to me, again.

"What the hell are you doing?" I was screaming.

He didn't seem shocked at all and quite calmly said to me, "Nobody needs to know."

I yelled again, "I would know, and Jesus Christ, you're my cousin!"

Psycho freak.

"What has happened to you? Have you completely lost your mind?"

What am I going to do now? I certainly am not going to continue this trip with you. There is something definitely wrong with you and I just wasn't aware of it.

I had to work to concentrate. I think I was in a complete state of shock.

"Beside the fact that we are cousins, you are married. I am married."

He didn't seem to care. He proceeded to tell me all the women he had already cheated on his wife with. *Didn't he see this as cheating?* I couldn't believe what he was telling me, let alone analyze what he was thinking. Has he cheated before? Has he raped other women before?

I don't know you at all. You must have worms eating your brain, but I need some help, and I need to get out of here.

Usually, when times were tough in my life, I would just pray, but I don't remember praying at this time. I went into survival mode of not wanting to poke the bear or anger him, even though I was raging inside. Even the next thing he did seemed strange.

He went into the bathroom and took a shower. I decided to walk out of the room. I just needed to get some air. I walked outside and then I walked into the main lobby of the hotel. I didn't really know where to go or what to do. I felt like I was just wandering around looking for an answer or some desperately needed guidance. What I really should have done was gather my things while he was in the shower and get the hell out of there.

Instead, I walked into the lobby and told the guy at the front desk that I was having some problems with my cousin without telling him what those problems were. I said I needed to get out of here and asked if they had any security. They didn't.

I went outside and called my husband. It was five in the morning by this time, and I knew I would wake Jeff up, but I didn't have a choice. I needed someone to talk to, and I needed some advice on what to do next. I told Jeff what had happened and that I was coming home. I also told him I was bringing my cousin with me. I believe we were both so stunned over my cousin's behavior, neither of us really knew what to do. Jeff's main concern was getting me home. I thought my cousin had lost his marbles and needed help, but how much danger was I willing to put myself in? I have never been a selfish person, and I wasn't going to start that day.

I know I was still in a total state of shock because I should have abandoned my cousin at that hotel and gotten the hell out of there. However, that is not what I did. I felt some kind of family obligation to him for reasons I still can't understand. I have always had a bit of fear for the males in my family and worried what would happen to me if I abandoned him there. What I did would make it harder for some other members of my family to believe me. I understand why: I might even feel the same way if it were someone else. However, I am not lying. I have never wavered on my story since the day it happened. I feel that should count a lot toward people finally deciding to believe me, but it may never happen.

One thing Theresa, my spiritual counselor, told me was that my cousin never meant to harm me and he never would have raped me. She told me that he truly had a thing for me and really wanted a relationship "like that" with me. Disturbing. However, this information brought me a little bit of comfort. Maybe my inner intuition knew I was safe and that's why I didn't turn my back on him. Personally, I think I was just in shock.

I told him we were heading back to Salem. Our trip was over. I drove him back to Salem, yelling at him the entire way. The majority of what I yelled at him was, "I am your cousin." I found the whole incident creepy, repulsive, and disrespectful. Just so darn disturbing. I ended up driving him to my parents' house. Privately, I told my father what happened and all dad said was, "OK, I will take care of it." I went

THIS DOES NOT LEAVE THIS HOUSE

home and immediately threw up in my kitchen sink. The people in my family who don't believe me say, "If he tried to rape you, why did you bring him back to Salem with you?" I completely understand why they think that, and I wonder why myself.

I think some part of me felt sorry for him. He is broken now, but he was also a person in my family whom I once cared about. For my entire life, I trusted this person. I have not spoken to him since the day I dropped him off at my parents. We could never be a family again after that, and I'm angry he took that from me. My father never spoke of it again either. It became yet another version of, "This does not leave this house."

I can definitely tell you who wasn't on my side: my mother, of course. I have never understood how a mother can treat her own children the way mine does. It sure doesn't feel like she loves me —never did.

A few years ago, my uncle put together a family reunion at a local park. My mother called to tell me about it and invited me to come. *Seems innocent enough, right?* I asked her if everyone in the family was invited, including the cousin who tried to rape me. She acted all innocent and said she hadn't given it any thought. *Really, Mom? This person tries to rape your own daughter and you hadn't "given it any thought?"*

"Well, can you please find out if he is going or not? And, if he is going, I request you don't go either out of loyalty to me."

Her response: "I have to go. If I don't go, everyone will be mad at me for not going."

OK, Queen of Sheba, you have to go. You're right. You've never had any loyalty to your own daughter, why start now?

Time draws near to the family reunion and Mom brings it up to me again. So, again I asked her if she knew if my cousin were going or not. She didn't know, and she didn't want to call anyone to find out. She actually got extremely angry with me when I told her I thought it was better for me if I didn't go. It surprised me how angry she was. She wouldn't stop yelling at me so I hung up on her.

Thanks for the support, Mom. You just go and have yourself a good time.

So, the day of the family reunion comes. Mom went to it; I did not. Turns out, he was there. Stephanie didn't go out of respect for me. I found out he was there because Stephanie found some photos on one of our cousins' Facebook page and told me about it. Curiosity got the better of me and I took a look at those pictures. What I saw shocked but did not surprise me. Sitting at a park picnic table was my mother, sitting directly across from him. Not only was she sitting with him, she appeared to be enjoying herself. How could she do that? How could she sit there appearing to have such a fun time laughing with him? Where's the loyalty?

Wait, it gets better . . .

Christmas day came around, and I felt obligated to invite my mother over to have Christmas dinner with us. I was having my daughter and my mother-in-law over as well. After dinner, we were all sitting in the family room chatting. Jeff was having a conversation with his mother. This was my mother's opportunity to strike.

Mom looked at me and whispered, "Have you seen the pictures on Amy's Facebook page yet?"

"Yes, Mom, I have seen them," I answered. "And for your information, they gave me one of my more intense panic attacks." Why was she whispering to me again?

This reminded me so much of how she used to whisper in my ear when I was a kid and it was never anything good. She saw that Jeff and his mother weren't paying any attention to her and were deep in a conversation, and she knew this would be her chance to mess with me.

But why, Mom? Why do you want to mess with me? More importantly, why do you not love me? Why have you always wanted to bring me such sadness and despair? What do you get out of treating me this way?

These questions have never really been answered for me. My dear aunt used to tell me, "Jules, your mother is jealous of you," then add, "Your mother is also competing against you for your father's attention." Was my aunt right? Part of me believed she was. You really can't pick your parents, can you?

I was upset after Mom said that to me about the Facebook pictures, so I got up and left the room to go find Stephanie. Stephanie was laying on my bed, chatting with some of her friends on her phone. I asked her why she was there and she said she had to get away from her grandma for a while. She was driving her crazy. So, I proceeded to tell Stephanie what Mom had just done to me. Right then, Jeff came into the room looking for me.

Stephanie said, "Jeff, time for Grandma to leave."

I told Jeff what Mom had said to me, and then Jeff walked out of the bedroom, walked up to my mother, and said, "Time for you to go home now."

She simply said, "I was waiting for that to happen."

Well, gee, Mom. If you knew what you were saying to me was bad enough to get you kicked out of my house on Christmas, then why in the world did you even say it to me?

She is way more diabolical than even I gave her credit for.

❦ 16 ❧

One of the more important things in my life has been my ability to listen to my gut—intuition, really, but I call it "my gut." I do believe I would have handled things much differently if only I had taken the time to listen to my gut. There have been times in my life, however, when I did take the time to listen, and some of those times have even saved my life.

When I was twenty-one, a few of my friends invited me to join them at a local bar called "The Oregon Museum." This was a bar frequented by many of my friends, but I hadn't been there yet. It was Thursday night, *Ladies Night*. There was a new breakout band called "Jenny and the Jeans" performing that night, and everyone was going. I felt like something was telling me not to go so I listened and stayed home.

That night, I went to bed right at 11:00 p.m. Every night before bed, I turned on the radio and listened to relaxing music to help me fall asleep. I had just turned on the radio in time to hear breaking news. I couldn't believe what I heard.

There had been a shooting at the Oregon Museum tavern. There were some casualties reported, but no real details yet. I jumped out of bed and ran downstairs. So many of my close friends were in that bar, and I should have been there. I laid awake all night listening for news of the welfare of the people in that building. So many people were in the bar that night. The shooter was a man, and he had just walked into the bar and started shooting the place up. Luckily, none of my friends were killed, but five of them were injured. At the end of the melee, four people were killed and twenty were injured. We never found out the motive for the shooting. I was thankful in the end that I didn't go that night. I had listened to my gut, and I will never regret it.

Theresa told me I have been a gifted empathic medium since the age of five. However, I believe this ability grew from my near-death experience when I was fifteen. I truly believe when I floated out of my body and up to the corner of that room I got close to a portal or a veil —the veil between our world and the next. My body was healed, and I was left with a very unlikely gift: the ability to communicate with spirits.

Well, I see them and hear them more than directly communicate. These experiences have been frightening, funny, and just downright incredible. Shocking and awesome all at the same time. My very first spirit was when I was sixteen, about a year after my out-of-body experience. I was sitting in the living room of our house nestled in a wooded area with dimmed lights, leaning against a rather large cabinet record player, listening to some of my favorite music. I have a real love for music, and it always enabled me a chance to escape my stressful life.

On this particular day, I was totally relaxed and not thinking of a thing. On the other side of the room, a soldier appeared—not just any soldier, but a very proud and dignified soldier holding his gun. I could see him as clearly as I could see anybody, except he was transparent. I instantly knew he was a spirit.

We shared a moment of intense eye contact and I couldn't move a muscle. I was frozen in place, completely engaged eye to eye with this proud spirit. I don't know how long he stayed there, but it felt like an eternity. He never changed his expression—not smiling, not frowning, just looking straight into my eyes as proudly as could be. He was holding his gun upright with the butt of the gun sitting on the ground. He was wearing a blue uniform, double-breasted with gold buttons, with a taller hat but not a stovepipe. He wore black, shiny boots with his blue pants tucked inside them. He was stunning. I couldn't possibly look away. He was strikingly handsome, appearing to be in his mid-twenties.

It got extremely cold in the room where I saw my soldier. I finally ran out of the room, opened the door to the family room, and ran inside. My entire family was there watching television. I stood there wide-eyed looking at them until finally someone broke the silence and asked me what my problem was.

"Is it cold in here?" I asked. "Someone should go into the other room and tell me if it's cold in there."

They all ignored my request, told me to be quiet, and continued watching TV. I was too scared to leave the room so I sat down, quietly reflecting over what had just happened to me.

A while later, I looked up the uniform he wore and discovered it was that of a Union soldier worn during the Civil War. *Amazing.* But why was he in my living room? I live in a small town in Oregon. *There weren't any Civil War battles in my area*, I remember thinking. Years later, I was told by a historian that there actually were a couple of Civil War battles in our area, and they happened to have taken place right in my neighborhood. *How could I ever share this remarkable experience with another person?*

My spirit guide here on earth is named Theresa. She is an empathic healer, a medium, as well as a counselor. She told me that it's very common when people see spirits for the first time for it to often be a soldier. I wish everyone had an opportunity to talk to Theresa. She's incredible. She is the reason I am writing this book. She has helped me shed so much light on what was always something that made me feel different, afraid, and a bit of a freak.

Especially in high school, the last thing I wanted to be was a medium. I didn't want to be different from my friends. I remember a teacher I had in high school discovered I could see auras. She was in awe, but I was embarrassed. I needed my friends. They were my "love supply." I couldn't risk them abandoning me by finding out I was different. I hid my abilities and, in doing so, I think I squelched them a lot. However, I still have them, and sometimes it can be quite frightening.

One day, I took Jeff to the cemetery to show him where some of my family members are buried. Some of them have very funny names, so I was going to show Jeff where they were. We were walking around, marveling at the age and beauty of some of the headstones, when I suddenly noticed, in the corner of the cemetery, a person wearing a long wool coat with the hood up. It kind of looked like a monk. (*Monks scared the crap out of me when I was a kid*). Their head was bent down like they were looking down at the ground or praying. I just stood there amazed at how someone would be wearing a long wool coat on a day that was almost 100 degrees outside. The head started to slowly raise up in my direction so I looked away, afraid of what I might see. My husband was with me and he didn't see it. I was so terrified that we left right away and I haven't been back since.

I told Theresa about this one day and she just calmly said to me, "That's a cemetery guardian. They aren't supposed to interact with people." I can't explain how mysterious this stuff is to me, but it gives me so much peace knowing there's something after we die. Death is not the end. For all the science geeks and skeptics out there, this is why: One of the most basic laws of science is the "Law of the Conservation of Energy." Energy cannot be created or destroyed; it can only be changed from one form to another.

Or . . . you can just take my word for it!

The most alarming things that happen to me are the things that happen in my own home, especially when I am there alone. I have had it explained to me like this: I am like a lighthouse, a beacon, for spirits. They know I can see and hear them, so they are drawn to me. Good, bad, any kind of spirits. I have learned that people are the same after they die as they are when they are alive. If they are real jerks or pranksters when they are alive, chances are they will be the same way when they are dead. Most of them also know they are dead, but they don't seem necessarily bothered by it. My house can be a revolving door of spiritual activity. I have had to lay down some ground rules like: don't scare me or wake me up when I am asleep, and don't appear when I am on the toilet or stare back at me from my mirror. *Please, just don't scare me.*

Seems to work most of time.

However, I have encountered some not-so-nice things before, too. Things I would consider diabolical or, perhaps, even demonic. Growls are terrifying when directly in your ear and unattached to anything physical. I have also had spirits mimic others in my house. One day, while sitting on my couch, I heard the backdoor open. Then I heard footsteps walking up the hallway and finally my husband's voice calling out my name. After waiting the appropriate amount of time for him to reach the end of the hallway, he never appeared. *Goosebumps.*

Another day, I was watching Stephanie's dogs, Lilly and Jax. Lilly likes to bark, and she was going crazy barking at something. Usually, they are very interested in the coat closet. I have often wondered if there is a portal in there. I have seen a little girl run in and out of there many times. I started yelling at Lilly to stop barking and she was completely ignoring me. Finally, I heard a voice out of nowhere that sounded exactly like Stephanie's say, "Lilly!" with a sternness that got her to stop barking immediately. That was freaky.

I used to think that we just happened to move into a haunted house and it had nothing to do with me. However, we moved into a new home and we were the first owners. If anything, it would have to be something with the land, but I have never had any luck researching it. The weirdest things still happen there. I have wanted to move on multiple occasions, but now I know there really isn't anywhere to go because the issue lies with me. These things will happen to me no matter where I live. It's not the place. It's me. It's a weird thing to have to come to terms with, but I finally did and I'm not nearly as scared as I used to be. I believe there is a reason I have this gift, so maybe I am supposed to embrace it and be grateful. *Not everyone gets to see spirits*, I tell myself.

My husband is still a bit of a skeptic even though things have happened to him in our house, too, on a much lesser scale than I experience. He has had his shirt tugged on, and he has heard my voice call his name when I wasn't even in the house. Even though he has had these things happen, he still finds a way to try to debunk it. I think it is just because he's a guy, and guys are very skeptical. I just tell him that's what you get for marrying a witch.

I still haven't figured out how something like this could happen. I keep a Bible on the mantle above the fireplace in the living room. The mantle was painted white and, when we moved in, there was red writing on the shelf that looked like red crayon. We couldn't exactly make out what it said, but it looked something like "mad dog" or "red dog." We painted over it, but it kept reappearing through the paint. I had to paint over it multiple times. I thought maybe a prankster child in the neighborhood somehow got in and wrote that, but how? Our house was completely secure and there really wasn't any way for a kid to get in there.

So, just to keep everything safe and positive in there, I keep a Bible on the mantle. One day, I walked into the living room and the Bible wasn't on the mantle anymore. It was lying open on the floor. I reached down, picked it up, and wondered how the Bible was now on the floor. I also wondered if there were a specific reason why it was open to these exact pages. Maybe there is a message here, so I decided to sit down and read the pages. Halfway through, to my amazement, was my maiden name written on one of the pages. I couldn't believe it. What are the odds that the Bible would fall and open up to the page with my name on it? Coincidence? I don't think so. I really don't believe in coincidences. This was intentional, and to this day I am in complete amazement at how this could have happened. There is just so darn much that science cannot explain.

I'm happy to say that today I am feeling a lot more at peace with the things that occur inside or outside of my house. I used to be convinced that there were negative, possibly demonic, spirits there. I still have a very strong faith in God, and God is stronger than anything negative. What I have learned to do is just pray when things get scary and that usually takes care of it for me.

Where could I turn for help? I used to feel so completely alone and wondered if I were going crazy at times. You don't just open the yellow pages and find someone to explain why things are so weird in your house. You don't just talk to your neighbors about this either. We have had so many different next-door neighbors over the years. We even had one family move out in the middle of the night. I'm sure there is something going on with the land that I have yet to figure out, but, for right now, things are comfortable, so I am just going to let it be.

The best advice I can give is to try not to get too scared because that fear energy feeds whatever might be there and gives it more strength. Also, just pray and ask God for help. My favorite prayer is, "St. Michael the Archangel." There is a force out there much stronger than us and waiting to help us, so don't hesitate to call upon it because they will come.

17

Anytime that you are afraid, or for anything that you're really afraid of, that's when you have to get up and face it because fear can hold you back. It took me a year to get out of my abusive marriage due to fear. He said he would kill me if I ever left him, and I was sure he meant it. However, I really should have left a lot sooner than I did. Luckily for me, things transpired and the stars aligned in the perfect way for me to make my escape. I remember a saying I liked when I was in high school: "Take life as it happens, but make it happen the way you want to take it." That is some good advice I wish I took more often.

I am terrified to fly but somehow I still do it. I have even been prescribed anxiety meds to calm my fears, but they never worked. I used to love to fly until one scary flight about a month after 9/11. We had been in the air for about an hour when the pilot announced we were going back to the airport due to engine problems. Scary enough, but then the lights began to flicker. The pilot came back on to inform us we were also having electrical problems. I was really scared, but my fear increased when I heard other passengers crying. It only took twenty minutes to get back to the airport. When we started coming down to land, I saw fire trucks and ambulances lining the runway. This terrified me even more so I prayed.

Our plane landed perfectly. We sat out on the runway for what felt like forever before we were cleared to taxi up to the airport. I got off the plane, went into the bathroom, and threw up. When I came out of the bathroom, my husband told me it was already time to line up to get on another flight. *No way am I getting back on another plane this soon. I'm taking a bus home.* My poor husband had to hold onto my arm to ensure I didn't run out of the nearest exit. I still make myself fly because I feel I will miss out on so much if I don't. I think it's very important to face and conquer your fears whenever you can.

I am especially afraid to write a tell-all about my life and the repercussions it could bring. Even as I write these words, there is a level of anxiety and a feeling that I am risking something, or there could be some level of punishment when it's all over. However, if my experiences help another person champion their own life in this world, then it was worth it. I will push past these inner fears and, when it is all said and done, I hope there will be healing. Doing this is terrifying; memories can be painful. Having the strength to go through it all again and relive it is a huge accomplishment. I used to think I should close the door to my past and never reopen it. Now I've opened it and it feels like freedom.

I have felt like the black sheep of my family for a very long time. Now that I have my loving husband and daughter, I don't feel that way anymore and it's a wonderful feeling. As I write this, I occasionally wonder if any of my family members will ever read it. I wonder if they might like it and think better of me, or not. Still looking for acceptance and equality. Time will tell how everything turns out. Maybe this will be a blessing that brings everyone together, or maybe it's necessary for my personal purging of all the ugliness in my past. My personal journey. My hope is that someone out there in the world is genuinely helped by what I have shared. That for me would be success. If there is one single person going through an abusive relationship and my experience gave them hope and an exit strategy, that is success. Take my story and heal from it.

One time, my father came to talk to me about something that was bothering him. We sat down and Dad began to talk. I was shocked, not only by what I was hearing but also because my father decided to share it with me. He proceeded to tell me that his younger brother, John, told him that his kids would never turn out like my father's kids did. I couldn't believe he said this to my dad. I have always loved and admired my Uncle John. I thought he liked me, too, but now I know the truth. He thinks my brother and I are losers. This hurt me deeply. I am not sure why my father chose to share this with me either. He had to have known this information would hurt me.

Gee, Dad. Did you forget that children tend to be considered a reflection of their parents?

Are you only supposed to judge people based on their careers and their professional achievements? I disagree. I judge people based on how they treat me. My message to my uncle is this: "You may think you walk on water, but you can't do it without a Bible in one hand and a bottle of scotch in the other. Just saying, you're a hypocrite. Clean up your own backyard before you judge mine."

A lot of things I've been through in my life have made me feel so alone. Nobody else could possibly know what this feels like. Or else, I hope nobody else has to suffer like this. My painful illnesses. Nobody else could possibly know what this feels like. Being a child in an abusive home. Having no voice. Having nowhere to go and nobody to turn to. Nobody else knows what this feels like. Being brutally raped and then treated like garbage by the hospital staff.

I hope nobody else knows what this feels like. If you have experienced anything like my experiences, I stand with you. You are not alone. You are not the rape. You are not the abuse. You are not the illness. No matter what it is, you are not that thing you carry around. You are a special person with a sensitive soul who deserves to be acknowledged. You are never alone. I stand with you.

Not worthy, not valued, not loved. These are all labels we give ourselves. These are labels more often given to us by the people who are supposed to love us. These are labels that stick in your psyche. In my case, I did not choose these labels, but sadly I was given them by an ex-husband and an unloving parent. I have had a lifetime of feeling unloved from the one woman who was supposed to love me unconditionally. You are not your illness, or your rape, or your abuse. It's time to change the negative label you unwittingly gave yourself. For me, it was like a constant tape on a loop repeating how worthless I was. Change the rhetoric and stop the stinkin' thinkin'. Please, just change the damn tape.

I have to remind myself to stop rolling my eyes if someone tells me I'm pretty. Stop refusing to believe it. This is all negative crap that needs to be disposed of. Accept the compliment and realize you have gifts, but, most of all, realize you have value in the world. If anyone treats you like you are less than perfect, rid your life of them. Put together a circle of people who build you up, not tear you down. Demand kindness and respect from people. My father really tried to help build my self-esteem by telling me, "You are not hamburger. You are steak."

My smartass answer back was, "OK, Dad, but that still makes me a piece of meat."

❧ 18 ❧

I believe I would have made a wonderful doctor. I'd wanted that since I was eleven years old, and everything I did was with that career in mind. Every penny I earned was put away for college. My father made it clear he was paying for my brother to go to college, but he wouldn't pay for me too. He actually told me that it was more important for my brother to go to college. I could "just get married." Perhaps people who become successful had supportive parents who encouraged them. I knew early on I wouldn't have financial help, mainly because I was the wrong gender. I wasn't going to have any support or encouragement, and my father never wavered on telling me so. I'm sure if I had been born a boy, it would have been completely different.

Every high school class that I could take as a college credit for medicine I took. I remember being so excited when I got the letter telling me that I was accepted for the pre-med program at the University of Oregon. I worked so hard for many years to accomplish this goal only to let the rape scare me away from college and bury my dreams. I am not, however, surprised the rape affected me like this. It is a very tragic and scary experience. I think the worst part was when I finally got the strength to tell my parents about it and they chose not to believe me. Even my brother was shocked by their reactions. We never spoke about it again. I still can't wrap my head around their lack of caring.

One evening, my husband and I were watching the 2016 Academy Awards show on TV. Lady Gaga was performing her song, "Till It Happens to You," from the movie *The Hunting Ground*. The movie was about rape on college campuses. I have not seen the movie, but the song was incredibly moving, and I sat there with tears running down my face. I looked over at my husband and he had tears streaming down his face too, not even trying to hide it from me. At that moment, it hit me. I was so touched because I realized after all these years, nobody had ever really cried for me. It meant so much to me, and I felt a sense of healing. How do you sufficiently thank someone when something they do touches you so deeply in your soul?

I strongly believe if the traumas we experience in life enable us to have the compassion and understanding to help someone through their trauma, then it somehow makes it worth it. I was working one night in the Emergency Room when a young girl was brought in by ambulance. I was assigned to admit her to the hospital, and it was then I realized what she was brought in for. She had been brutally raped on the Willamette University campus. This poor girl was too hysterical to even give us her name. I stood beside her and calmly tried to talk to her. She was beyond consoling.

"I'm so sorry." I told her. "I know what you're going through."

She started screaming at me. "How dare you say that to me!" She yelled. "You do not know what I am going through!"

I didn't get upset with her. She had every right to feel the way she did. I desperately wanted to help this girl because I saw myself there on that hospital bed. After I was able to calm her enough to explain I had also been raped and that mine too was brutal, she started to cry. This had been her first sexual experience, too. Her pants were also soaked in blood, just like mine had been. I was so grateful when I was able to help calm her and helped get her through this process. She trusted me. We had a bond and a connection I wish nobody ever had to have.

I am grateful I was eventually able to help her. I remember the nurse yelling at me to relax when I had to go through my rape exam. I will put her in the "burned-out nurse" category. I feel so blessed that I had been able to help this girl who came into my hospital that night. It is sad and tragic that we both had to experience such trauma, but I felt fortunate I was there to help her through hers.

Even though we probably don't always consciously deal with our past traumas, I strongly believe somehow our subconscious minds and bodies are still dealing with it. I have often wondered if all this stress is what has brought on the pancreatitis that I now deal with chronically. I have been told the area where my pain is happens to be the control chakra. I rarely felt in control of anything, including my own thoughts as a child. I was constantly told how to act, what to think, and how to feel.

Pancreatitis is such a scary and painful condition. I'd never heard of it before I had it. It is the most physically painful thing I have ever had to deal with. Kidney infections are very painful too, but nothing comes close to the pain associated with pancreatitis. When I first met Theresa, the first thing she did was place her hand directly on the spot on herself where my pain is located. Then she looked at me in total disbelief and said, "Unspeakable pain." She said usually the spirits will allow her to experience what a person is feeling, even if it is just for a brief moment, but in my case, they wouldn't let her feel it.

I suffered terribly for three months before I was finally diagnosed. I was constantly doubled over on the floor in agonizing pain, going from one doctor to another and in and out of the emergency room. This first episode was terrifying because nobody could figure out what was wrong with me and I was beginning to think I was losing my mind. My husband got so frustrated with the medical community in our town that he drove me to a hospital an hour away in Portland. Turns out nobody in my town had run the appropriate tests yet.

When the correct test was finally performed in Portland, I was diagnosed with pancreatitis and admitted to the hospital. I would stay there for an entire month attached to a feeding tube. I had become extremely malnourished. Food is the enemy with pancreatitis, and the best thing to do is to just stop eating and let the pancreas rest. I had stopped eating already because I was too sick and couldn't keep anything down. Plus, anything I ate caused me more pain.

The number one cause of pancreatitis, I found out, is alcoholism. I kept wondering why everyone on the medical staff at the hospital constantly asked me how much alcohol I drank. I don't drink and haven't in a very long time so they had to search for another reason. What they eventually discovered was that a gallstone had lodged in my pancreas causing damage to my pancreas. They removed my gall bladder, but by that time it was really too late. The damage was done.

I remember one day in the hospital hearing a patient down the hall screaming. I asked my nurse what was going on and who was torturing the patient down the hall. She told me they were giving them a feeding tube. This was right before they gave me mine. It was so creepy. The nurse looked at me with a sinister smile and said, "We will be placing your feeding tube soon." At least some of the people who took care of me had a sense of humor.

Humor has gotten me through a lot of very dark days in my life. It took them four tries before they got my feeding tube in the right spot. I wouldn't say it was excruciatingly painful, and I didn't scream at all with mine, but it is uncomfortable. I was so relieved when, a couple of years ago when I needed a feeding tube again, the doctor took pity on me and gave me conscious sedation so I wasn't aware of what was happening.

I recovered from my first episode and went a full two years pain-free. I woke up on Thanksgiving morning feeling like I had a really intense case of the flu. Later that day, the intense pain set in and I knew for sure it was pancreatitis. We had already invited a large group of people over for Thanksgiving dinner, so Jeff handled all the cooking and I stayed in bed. We didn't feel right cancelling Thanksgiving on the same day. I was eventually hospitalized for a couple of weeks. I recovered and went another two years free of pancreatitis, then I had another attack. This last time, however, it didn't go away, and now my diagnosis is chronic pancreatitis. The pain has not gone away in over two years.

Occasionally, I have to stop eating and use a feeding tube so my pancreas can rest. I really appreciate what a gift food is now. When you take something for granted like eating, and then your body can't do it anymore, you really miss it. I have so much compassion for people who have to use a feeding tube all the time. Food just tastes so darn good, and I really miss it when I can't have it. However, it's an easy decision not to eat when food equals intense pain.

I had a flare-up right after we purchased season tickets for the Portland Trailblazers. Our seats were in the private club section where the food was included with the price of the tickets. I had a feeding tube and couldn't eat any of the food there. I was also very self-conscious. People don't mean to stare, but trust me, they stare. They stare a lot, and they give you these intensely sympathetic looks. I don't even think they realize they are looking at you like that, but it also showed me how much people cared and felt for me.

I have gone about three years without needing another feeding tube, but I have to be very careful with what I eat. Sometimes I look at whole sections in the grocery store and realize I can't eat any of it. The doctors have talked to me about placing a permanent feeding tube in my stomach but, luckily, I have managed to fight that off so far. I don't want to lose hope that I will be healed someday either. I had one miracle in my life; I could have another one. Miracles happen every day.

I can see how a person with this, or any other chronic illness, can become depressed, but my advice is don't ever stop fighting. It's very important to stay positive. My illness can be fatal, and I am reminded of this every time a TV commercial for some drug comes on. I cringe when I hear, "This may lead to pancreatitis, which can be fatal."

I also suffer from a muscle disease called fibromyalgia. When I was in my mid-thirties, I was involved in a hit-and-run car accident. A Pontiac Trans Am ran a red light going about fifty miles per hour and broadsided my car. The impact caused my car to spin on dry pavement. I hit another car and totaled it and didn't even realize I had hit it until someone told me. My car came crashing into the side of the curb and I just sat there, frozen. A man ran over to my car, opened my door, and told me I needed to get out of the car right away. He was afraid it could catch fire with me in it. I didn't want to get out of the car, however, because the impact had caused my bra to break. *How the heck does an impact break a bra?*

He helped me out and I collapsed on the grass next to my car. I thanked him for stopping to help me, and that is when he told me I hit his car. Everything happened so fast. I had no idea I'd even hit another car. The Trans Am that hit me never stopped. Luckily, a witness was able to get the license plate number. While I was being lifted into the ambulance, a police officer came over and told me they knew who hit me because he was already wanted. He was a drug dealer who sold drugs up and down the west coast from here to Mexico. I'm pretty sure that's why he didn't stop.

I was diagnosed with fibromyalgia a year after the accident. I was told I had the worst case the doctor had ever seen. He also told me that I would be confined to a wheelchair someday. Why he chose to tell me this, I don't know, but, luckily, I am not in a wheelchair today. I think little was known about fibromyalgia back then. It mainly feels like flu symptoms with the all-over body aches associated with the flu. Cold and rain affect me terribly, so most winters I ache all the time. I get a nice break from it in the summer when it's warm.

It's a pretty miserable, achy illness to have, and I feel for all who suffer with it. When I was first diagnosed, I was told it was a muscle disease. Lately, I am hearing it's an illness caused by mental stress and/or childhood trauma.

I had another hit-and-run accident in 2015. We were stopped at a stoplight. When the light turned green and the car ahead of me started to proceed, a strong gust of wind came up, pulled the entire back window out of their car in one big piece, and it came crashing down on the driver's side of my car. It slid down the entire left side of my car causing a ton of damage. They obviously knew this had happened, but they chose to turn the corner, hit the gas, and disappeared.

Again, how could they just leave me there and not wonder if I were OK? Luckily for me, the glass landed on the side of my car instead of crashing through my front window. That could have killed me. I do believe I have guardian angels watching over me. There have been many times in my life I could have been seriously injured or killed, yet

I came out of it remarkably unscathed. We all have spirit guides and guardian angels watching over us. Knowing this gives me peace.

I have had a couple other experiences I would also relate to as divine assistance. I was driving on a very windy road up in the mountains. I was coming around the corner too fast and almost went off the edge of the cliff. If I had driven off the edge, I would have certainly died because the drop-off was incredible. It was as if I could feel my car go off the edge and then it was somehow gently placed back onto the road. It was just exactly like that, and I can't find any other way to explain it.

Another time, I was driving in snow and ice late at night. I needed to turn onto a street that went up a hill. Right after I turned onto the street, my car hit a patch of ice and slid into the ditch on the wrong side of the road. It's completely dark with no streetlights in this location. Any cars that might be coming down the hill wouldn't be able to see me and would certainly run right into me. To this day, I can't explain how this happened.

I got out of my car, grabbed the door, and pushed my car out of the ditch. I am not a bodybuilder or weight lifter of any kind. I am only five-foot-one-*and-a-half* inches tall and I weigh about 110 pounds. How in the world did a lightweight like me rescue my car as well as myself off that road? I believe it was divine intervention.

What else could it have been?

❧ 19 ❧

I t amazes me, all the times my mother whispered in my ear, how I was going to find her dead, yet she never once went through with it. *Coward*, I used to think. I realized early on that all she was really after was attention. She was too in love with herself to ever go through with it. Plus, she had stolen all my self-esteem early on, so she was in good shape. She thought she was gorgeous, slender, stylish, and downright breathtaking. People like that don't kill themselves; they just make everyone around them miserable instead.

However, I began to think that one way to handle sadness and struggles in life was just to end that life. As if suicide were really an option. Isn't that what my mother had always taught me? Every time she creepily whispered in my ear how I was going to find her dead, my mother was teaching me without even realizing it that this was one coping strategy to consider. *Well, she always considered it*, I thought, *but she was really lousy at ever accomplishing it.*

I had been dating a police officer for a little over a year. We met a couple years after my divorce. We had a really good time together and I thought we were in love. We had already started talking about marriage. He was a good person, hard worker and not a heavy drinker, which is one of my main requirements. He was just very dependable. I think I was looking for a companion for me, but more importantly, I was looking for a dependable father for Stephanie.

One night, we had plans to go out to dinner and then to a movie. We went back to his house and I decided to spend the night. We got into bed, and that's when he lowered the boom on me.

"I don't think this is going to work out." His tone was matter-of-fact.

"Wait." I couldn't believe what I was hearing. "What?"

He just repeated himself. "I don't think this is going to work out."

I said, "This, what?"

He answered again, casually. "Us. I don't think we are going to work out."

I laughed. This must be a joke.

He wasn't laughing with me.

The moment it hit me that he was really serious, I jumped out of bed.

"You had to wait until we got into bed to tell me this?" *Talk about timing.* I didn't give him a chance to answer. I was so shocked, hurt, and, most of all, insulted.

Was dinner and the movie my parting gift?

I got dressed and left his house. It's so weird the things we do when we are stressed out. It was around two in the morning and I went and got gas for my car. I must have been really stressed out because I didn't even need gas. I couldn't believe what had just happened. Instead of heading home, I drove back to his house and let myself in. He met me at the door and told me to give him my key back.

"You shouldn't just walk in," he told me. "I'm a cop. I have guns and I could accidentally shoot you."

He's worried he might accidentally shoot me?

I gave him my key, but I needed an explanation. He refused to tell me anything, then he asked me to leave because he needed to get some rest.

There is always a reason when you are breaking up with someone, so be a gentleman and tell me why.

I spent the next six months in the dark as to what the real reason was and he continued to lead me on. He would call me, I would go over to see him, make him dinner, get my hopes up, then get let down again. I was on a never-ending rollercoaster.

Finally, one of the other police officers he worked with took pity on me and told me the reason. My on-again, off-again boyfriend had another girlfriend. She was a police officer, too, and they had been seeing each other for over eight months. I was crushed. He didn't have the balls to tell me the truth, but he sure didn't mind using me and leading me on either. I confronted him and he didn't deny it. I finally gave up. However, I didn't realize all the damage that had already been done to me. I had fallen into depression.

Stephanie was almost three at the time. One night after work, I picked up some beers on the way home because I had invited a couple of friends over for drinks. I wasn't a big drinker, but the people I had invited over were. I had been having a lot of panic attacks, so my doctor put me on medication to help me relax. I ended up drinking too much, started feeling even more depressed, then started to play with a razor.

I began cutting my wrist. I don't really know why I was doing this, but I remember I didn't feel anything. *Could this be making me feel better? Shouldn't this be painful as hell?* In that moment, I felt a sense of peace. I felt myself fading into numbness. I would finally be safe, pain-free and . . . alone.

Wait! Through my fog, I could see Stephanie asleep in her bed. I thought, *What the hell am I doing? How could I allow my precious girl to wake up and find her mommy dead?*

I realized that something was terribly wrong with me and I needed to get some help. I looked up the crisis hotline number in the phone book and dialed.

Stephanie didn't know it, but she saved me that night.

It was probably around five in the morning when I finally made the call for help. I talked to the sweetest lady. We talked for a while, then she asked me if she could come over to my house. Something about her made me completely trust her and I really needed her to help me.

When she arrived, she talked me into letting her take me to the hospital. I woke Stephanie up and she came with us. This angel of mercy stayed with Stephanie in the waiting room while I admitted myself into the emergency room for treatment. Luckily, I didn't need stitches, but to this day I still have the scar, and I am glad. It is a reminder to me where I never want to go again. I don't think I really intended to take my life that night, but it was definitely a cry for help.

The hardest part was the fact that I had worked in the emergency room and everyone there knew me. One of the kinder doctors in the ER came in to treat me. When he looked at me all, he said was, "Oh, Julie." He convinced me to admit myself to the hospital for evaluation and I agreed. I needed to take care of a few things first, like who was going to watch Stephanie, but I would be back.

Luckily, Mom and Dad offered to watch Stephanie and I returned that very same day and admitted myself to the hospital. I desperately wanted to get better so I listened to everything they told me and I did everything they said. It's really not that surprising I had a suicide attempt.

When I think back, there were so many times my mother pounded into my head, over and over again, that this was the only way to cope. I started to believe this was an option and a way out when there is a lot of darkness in your life. I also thought I would show her it could be done. What was I going to prove? That I could make myself dead? That is so scary to me now when I think about it. Suicide is a permanent solution to a temporary problem. How does taking your life fix anything?

My uncle decided to make this a learning opportunity and brought his two children to visit me at the mental hospital. I knew instantly it wasn't out of the kindness of their hearts or compassion for me. No, it was meant to show their kids what "not" to do. I wasn't being supported—quite the opposite. I was on display. It reminded me a lot of how I used to feel in Catholic school: humiliated. Again, is it any wonder I had issues?

I am happy to say I am all better now, and I have never thought of suicide as a coping mechanism since. I lost my job at the hospital shortly after this happened. The previous month, I had a perfect review and my attendance record was also perfect. I was told upon my termination that I was fired due to lack of attendance. *Talk about kicking a person when they are down.* I was devastated. I was still in a fragile state and now I have just lost my job. I really liked working there; however, being there for four years was probably not the healthiest environment for someone as empathetic as myself. I brought a lot of sadness home with me.

It was really time to move on, but how very cruel of them to fire me. I probably could have sued them, but I really didn't want the hassle. I also believe that when one door closes, another one opens. Sometimes even a better door opens. This was true in my case. Shortly after getting fired, I got a job as an assistant to the president of a mortgage company and went on to be a top-producing mortgage loan officer.

I loved my job as a mortgage loan officer. I was so proud of the "top producer of the month" awards I received. They made me feel so good, and for someone like me who's desperately in need of self-esteem, that's a big deal. Times were good, rates were low, and everyone was refinancing their home.

I made a deal with a realtor I knew who had just listed an entire subdivision near my home. He allowed me to prequalify potential customers at his open house on Sundays if I brought homemade cookies. I got a lot of customers from doing this. One thing I learned in business is that the more you bust your butt, the more profitable and successful you will become. I believe the open-house strategy got me the most business. The part of my job I loved the most were first-time home buyers. Usually, the husbands were mega stressed out and the wives were totally in love with the house and already making plans to decorate. I especially loved it when I could tell them they were approved.

It was a very rewarding career, and I finally found something I looked forward to every day. The only bad part: I was hardly home. This kind of business demands a lot of your time. Some days I would go to work at seven in the morning and come home at nine at night. That is not conducive for raising a family. My daughter was growing up and I was missing it. I really loved my job, but missing out on so much of Stephanie's life broke my heart. I began to wonder if there were another way to make money that would enable me to spend more time with her. I came up with an idea.

Unfortunately, it required I quit the job I had grown to love, but Stephanie needed me more. She was being bullied at school, and I couldn't get anyone to help me. I complained to the principal, her teacher, counselors, and everyone else who would listen. I even went to the bully's house, but her mother wouldn't listen to me either. All her mother said to me was, "My daughter said she's not doing anything to Stephanie, and children don't lie."

Oh, OK. My daughter is getting more and more depressed by the day and faking illnesses so she doesn't have to go to school, but by all means believe your daughter. FYI . . . kids lie.

Eventually, we bought another house in a different school district. I couldn't get any help, and the bullying was getting worse by the day. It was so frustrating. No matter how hard I tried, I couldn't get any help from anyone, anywhere. We decided our only option was to give up and move to a different school district. It was one of the most heart-breaking and intensely frustrating times in my life.

By this time, Jeff had built a profitable commercial janitorial business he had taken over from his father. To replace some of the income from my job as a loan officer, I offered to do some cleaning for the business. I didn't need a ton of money to be happy. I just needed enough to pay the bills and have a little fun. I talked it over with Jeff and he agreed. He said he had some accounts that I could clean and it might be enough income to get us by. These offices had to be cleaned during the day when people were still there, and those jobs are hard to staff. Most janitorial jobs are done at night when everyone has left for the day.

I cried on my last day at the bank. I had grown close to my coworkers, and we were like family. Now I'm a janitor. What a change, going from having my own office, my own secretary, and my own loan processor to cleaning toilets. Sometimes, people were downright cruel and demeaning. Some days, I wanted to scream at them that I used to be a mortgage loan officer or that I'm part owner of this janitorial company. I never did either one. However, it did give me a much better understanding about what our employees have had to deal with.

❧ 20 ❧

The greatest gift I was ever given was when my daughter thanked me for breaking "the cycle"—the cycle of abuse that so many people, I am finding out, never break. Wouldn't people want more for their children than they had? Especially if they were abused themselves?

What I am coming to learn is that it is just more natural for people to repeat cycles. I have heard the phrase "It's all they know" far too many times. If they were abused as children, they typically grew up to abuse their own children without giving it a second thought.

I never spanked Stephanie. I was too afraid of losing control and harming her. I was terrified that I would end up being just like my parents. I never forgot the fear I felt when my brother and I were being beaten, whether it was by our parents or from our Catholic school. I couldn't imagine doing that to my child. However, I am sure every parent out there who abuses their children couldn't imagine doing that either.

Imagine you are able to end the cycle of abuse in your own family and how incredible that is on so many levels. First of all, you don't have to feel guilty because you just lost control and beat your child out of anger. Now, wrap your mind around this awesomeness. You are the hero that broke the cycle of abuse in your family. Now your child is grown and has their own children. They will also benefit from the fact that you showed, through example, how to be a great parent. Then, their children will grow up and have children who will also benefit from not being abused. Then their children will benefit . . . and so on and so on throughout time. I love that I changed things in my family for the better for many generations to come. I don't think there is anything in the world that is more important.

Any religion that condones the abuse of children is disgusting and shameful. For me, this is the Catholic religion. Anyone who preys upon children are monsters. Those who hide behind God to do it are the worst kind. I remember wondering when I was little if this was OK with God. *Did God want me to get hit? Did he want me to hurt and cry? Why was God so mean? Why was I so bad that I needed to be paddled all the time? Am I really evil because I'm left-handed? I didn't mean to be left-handed. Why was I the only kid tied to my chair? I must be evil. No other kids are tied to their chair.*

I will never understand this mindset. Children are born innocent, not evil. This stuff crushes a child's self-esteem—*crushes* it. If it takes a village to raise a child, then it can also take a village to abuse and destroy one. I saw a video on TV of a five-year-old child getting paddled at his school. His mother filmed the entire thing. This was done to him by his teachers. His mother was told that if she didn't let them paddle him "only one time," her child would be kicked out of school. I would have pulled my child out of there so fast. I couldn't believe this was on TV, and I didn't know what horrible thing a five-year-old could have done to deserve that. His mother was supposed to be his warrior and get him out of there, not just stand there filming it. Not OK. I don't care what anybody says; it is not OK.

I was beaten many, many times, and, trust me, it stays with you. The paddle I got hit with had holes drilled into it. I wonder which nun came up with the bright idea to drill holes in it. Did they discover this would make it sting more? It definitely enabled the child to hear the paddle coming, that's for sure. I will always remember that sound. Why would anyone want to break the spirit of an innocent child? *Their little hearts won't heal.*

You can't really stuff your feelings because, one way or another, you have to deal with it or it comes out in other, more terrifying ways. For me, panic attacks are terrifying. Anyone who has ever dealt with them will understand exactly what I am talking about. If you haven't had to deal with them, consider yourself blessed.

I still get so angry when I look back on the way my parents treated me when they found out I was pregnant. Thank goodness, my life now is calm and, for the most part, drama-free. It was so hurtful when my mother tried to trick me into getting an abortion. Thank God, the doctor's office didn't perform abortions. My parents were all about how they looked to the neighbors, our extended family, and society as a whole. I stood my ground, carried my baby with pride, and never, ever regretted my decision. No matter what I do in my life, Stephanie will always be my greatest accomplishment. Even so, it would have really been nice to have had the love and support of parents excited about becoming new grandparents.

Mental note: don't ever let my child know what this feels like.

When Stephanie called me to tell me she was pregnant, I didn't believe her. I should consider myself lucky I didn't just get a text. It finally hit me that she wasn't joking when I heard her call out to her husband, "Jim, Mom doesn't believe me." I was driving at the time and immediately pulled the car off the road into a parking lot. It finally hit me that this was real.

"Why didn't you believe me, Mom?" Stephanie was speaking through the phone again.

In my silly, joking manner, I replied, "Because I haven't given you permission to do that yet."

Oh well, I was going to be a grandma. I smiled and cried off and on all day long. I floated around and dreamed of what it was going to be like. I already knew what kind of grandma I wanted to be. I wanted to be the same kind of grandma to Stephanie's baby that my Grandma Eva was to me. I embraced this new part of my life and showered my daughter with tears of joy and total support.

Stephanie will never know what it feels like not to have that.

❧ 21 ❧

I finally had to cut my mother loose from my life, and that was hard for me to do, especially considering my very Catholic upbringing. Even though I now think of myself as a "recovering Catholic," there are still a lot of things that have stayed with me over the years, like Catholic brainwash techniques that were drilled into our little psyches such as, "Spare the rod, spoil the child," or, my other favorite, "Thou shalt honor thy mother and thy father" stuff. They should have added some kind of disclaimer in there that stated, "Thou shalt honor them unless thy parents are bat-crap crazy soul suckers."

The last time I saw my mother was the day after Mother's Day, 2015. I had already pretty much decided to keep my distance from her out of the need to protect my own mental health and peace of mind. However, she still had a weird way of torturing me through other people. We had a major blowout that day, and it was very ugly and a little bit scary. Fighting with crazy usually is. Remember my brother? Because she cried to him, he sent me a very ugly text message as a result. Gotta hand it to her, she can be very convincing. He probably still doesn't know he was manipulated by her that day. It was still Mother's Day, and he was chastising me for not going to see our mother.

What about you, Steve? I'm not the only one of her children who doesn't want to have anything to do with her. Dear sweet brother of mine who moved all the way to Texas and stuck me out here with her, not to mention your own children you abandoned in Las Vegas, why don't you please move her to Texas and have her live with you, if you care so damn much? But, most of all, please don't stick your nose where it doesn't belong.

The thing about my brother is that he is just like my mother and can be downright nasty when he wants to be. I am a lot more like my father, and, when weighed against the alternative, I will take it. Mom and my brother tended to gang up on me a lot. My mother loved it when my brother made comments to me about my weight. He used to say things like, "If you want to be top-heavy, walk on your hands." Mom really laughed at that one. Her other favorite dig was when he called me a freak of nature.

I have had many friends over the years tell me if my mother were theirs, they wouldn't have anything to do with her. They couldn't understand why I continually put up with her abuse. It's mainly because I felt an obligation to my mother, but certainly not because we had any kind of relationship. I rarely shared my life with people I didn't know very well. However, occasionally I shared a few things with people I believed I could trust. It always surprised me how shocked others were at the stories I told them. It especially surprised me to see the looks on their faces. Their jaws would drop and they would just look at me in complete disbelief. I guess when you are as used to it as I was, it becomes your normal, but normal people are shocked by it. I used to think I should keep this stuff to myself because either people will think I'm the crazy one and just making this all up, or, worse, they would pity me.

Back to Mother's Day. My brother sent me an angry text blaming me for our mother not seeing Stephanie's baby yet. Here we go again: Mom has been talking to my brother about what a horrible daughter I am and it seems to be working. One thing I will say about my mother, she can be extremely convincing and can get anyone to believe the crazy things she says. People really buy into her propaganda. She can also dig information out of people before they even realize they are handing it over. I told my brother that whether I agreed with her decision or not, Stephanie is Eva's mother and it is completely her decision. In other words, none of my business or yours.

I was texting with Stephanie, so I sent her the part of my brother's text that was about her. Stephanie got pretty upset and called my brother. She is very defensive of me, and she wanted him to know that if he had anything to say about it, say it to her, not me. I really respect the kind of woman Stephanie has grown up to be. She doesn't take any crap off people like I have my entire life, and she is definitely not afraid to speak her mind.

Let's just say my brother was less than thrilled to have Stephanie, let alone any woman, stand up to him. My brother has serious anger issues. However . . .

You are my daughter's uncle. No matter what, you don't get angry and tell your niece to "go fuck herself."

Does it get any slimier than that? With him, it probably does, but that's quite enough for me. I really don't know him. I don't think I ever will. Obviously, I am very defensive for Stephanie and this really upset me. I never went over to see my mother that day. I went to spend the day with my daughter and granddaughter. It was Stephanie's first Mother's Day, and my mother had just tried to ruin it without even saying a word to her. She succeeded in getting my brother to do all her dirty work. There was a black cloud hanging over the rest of that day.

The next day I went to my mother's house. I wanted to discuss what happened the day before and let her know how horrible my brother was to her granddaughter. I have a key to her house, so, when she didn't answer the door, I let myself in. When I walked into the family room, even I was surprised at what I saw. There she was, standing in the middle of the room with the TV volume all the way down and acting like she was hiding from me.

"Mom, what's going on?"

Her first words to me were, "Get out of my house or I will call the police."

I said, "Go ahead. Call the police."

What is going on with you now?

I asked her why she wouldn't answer the door. She never answered me. She just kept telling me to get out. *Crazy was on a new level today*, I remember thinking. It felt so completely awkward just being there. Why was she trying to hide from me? Did she know what had taken place with my brother, so she already knew I was going to be upset? *Oh, I get it, her plan had worked.* She had this all planned like she had written the script for it or something.

Again, I found myself standing in the middle of my mother's home feeling like I was having another brush with evil. This time, I brought a recording device with me. I must have had a psychic moment that told me to bring a recorder and hide it in my purse. My mother was always denying her horrible acts and always denied the terrible things she said to me, so this time I was going armed with some proof. I would record our conversation so, when she denied everything, I would have it on tape.

I bit my tongue and proceeded to say, "Your son told your granddaughter to go fuck herself."

What did my mother do? She got this really creepy grin on her face and said, "Good."

OK, this is enraging me now. Good? *Good?* Did she just say, "Good"? Unbelievable.

"This is your granddaughter we are talking about, remember?"

She actually looked pleased that my brother had said that to her. So, I took a deep breath and went on. I was beyond angry at her, but I had more to say. I told her that Steve was also concerned that if I didn't do something to correct our relationship, I would feel guilty if she died. She proceeded to tell me she couldn't care less and, to top it off, she added that she wouldn't give a shit if I died.

Wouldn't "give a shit"?

Remember my pancreatitis issues? She told me if I died tomorrow from pancreatitis, she wouldn't care and then, again, she told me to get out of her house. Oh, but now she remembered I had a key to her house, so she asked me to put the key on the counter and then leave.

I was pissed.

"Nope, I am keeping the key," I answered her back.

"Oh, so you don't care that I will have to pay money to get my locks changed?"

What the hell, Mom? You just told me you didn't care if I died, but I'm supposed to care about your stupid locks? Oh, and by the way, why do you feel the need to change your locks? Because I'm such a criminal?

Jesus, am I in the Twilight Zone? Nope, you're just having another encounter with your psychotic mother.

Damn, it was just too much sometimes.

I told her I would be happy to leave but not until I got the two blankets my Grandma Eva had made for me when I was little. She went and got the quilts, came back, and threw them at me.

"I have a ring of hers," she added out of the blue. "Do you want it?"

"Sure." *What is happening now?*

Then she said she needed to go into her bedroom to get the ring, but I am to stay in the kitchen and not come into her room because she doesn't want me to see where she keeps her "valuables."

Again, what is going on with you, Mother?

It occurred to me at that moment, my mother doesn't know me at all. If she did know me, she would know how very unmaterialistic I am. My mother has a lot of high-end jewelry, all diamonds and gold, and I couldn't care less about any of it.

I am not a materialistic person because of you, Mother.

I walked right into the bedroom, completely ignoring her orders. She was trying to push me out of the room, and I realized I had better get out of there before things turned physical. I felt such hatred for my mother at that moment, but I didn't want to be put in a position of having to defend myself. I have never once hit my mother and I didn't plan to start today. She'd hit me more times than I will ever remember, but there is just something very taboo with hitting a parent. But hell, what do I know, I am suffering from a lifetime of brainwashing. Trust me, I have wanted to hit her many, many times, but I am proud I never did. Not that she didn't deserve it. She is freaking awful. This is one of those times when my father would have said those fateful words, "This does not leave this house," if he were still alive.

I needed to get the hell out of there, so I told her to keep the ring. I left her key on the counter. I wouldn't be needing it again, and I didn't really want it anyway. As I was walking away, she said something that really surprised me.

She looked at me and said, "I wish I had taped this to show everyone how horrible you are to me."

"I am taping it," I answered.

She didn't believe me and told me to prove it, so I did. I pulled the tape recorder out of my purse and showed it to her. She tried to grab it out of my hand, but I managed to pull away from her grasp.

"Mom, take a good look at my face because this is the last time you are ever going to see it."

She tried to grab me again, but I got away. I'm not sure what she was grabbing me for this time. I think maybe she was trying to hit me or scratch me like she had done so many times before. I walked quickly away from her and out of the front door. I slammed that door as hard as I could behind me, got in my car, and drove away. I was shaking so hard. I knew that was the last time I was ever going to see my mother. Her grabbing me was so reminiscent of other times when she had tried to keep me from leaving. One time, she scratched the back of my hands so badly I bled all over my car as I was driving away. But this time I was free. *I am going to stay free and not look back. Even if other people try to make me feel like shit because she has convinced them that I am a terrible daughter, I am staying free this time.*

Most of the time it feels really good, but sometimes it feels really sad.

Did I decide to cut her loose or did she finally run me off? I had to get away from all the toxicity and get my head on straight. I believe it took me longer than most people would have taken, but there's that Catholic guilt again. Even though I consider myself a recovering Catholic, I am still being influenced psychologically by it. Guilt is such a useless emotion. Trust me, I have a lot of experience with this emotion—it's useless.

I truly believe getting away from my mother and the constant criticism has done a world of good for my peace of mind and self-esteem. I tortured myself for many years, or, I should say I allowed my mother to torture me out of a sense of obligation. But, you eventually come to the point where enough is enough. I have been told I should have come to this place a long time ago, but later is better than never.

I settled for being treated like a second-class citizen and the abuse just became my normal. It is not OK for anyone no matter who they are to treat you badly. The part that really hurts is the realization that my mother never loved me. I have been told many times by people who know her that she didn't have the ability to love because she is mentally unstable. Whatever the reason, it's still the same conclusion and it still hurts.

I have yearned for a mother my entire life. I needed love from a mother so badly. I never once knew what it felt like to have a mother who unconditionally loved me, was on my side, or had my back. I especially couldn't ever trust her with anything, especially not my deepest secrets or desires. She was really good at digging information out of me or anyone else. I remember numerous times my girlfriends would apologize to me because they had told my mother something they knew I didn't want her to know. I never got mad at my girlfriends because I knew how masterful my mother was at getting information. How embarrassing to have your mother call your girlfriends to dig information out of them. I have lost count of the amount of times I had to apologize for my mother to, well, everyone. Funny thing is though, I was a really good kid. I never did drugs or smoked or got into serious trouble of any kind. I'm not trying to say I was a model child, but I never did anything worse than skipping class here and there.

When I let my guard down and thought maybe things were getting better and I could put a little trust in my mother were the times I regretted the most. She always used things against me. Any tiny bit of gossipy information she got on me was shared with anyone who would listen. The more detrimental to my reputation, the more enjoyable it was for her. I learned early in life that I couldn't trust her with anything and she wasn't on my side and probably never would be. This is a really tough thing for a child to learn.

Of course, because I yearned so badly for this, I kept trying to change my reality and desperately wanted to confide in her, but every single time I did, it backfired on me. I don't have one single memory of my mother ever apologizing to me for anything. What I remember her saying instead was, "I did not," or, "I never said that," or, "That never happened." So blatant and defiant were her denials. She had a magical way of making herself the victim. She always bragged to everyone about what an outstanding mother she was, too. It was like she was trying to convince herself. How many times have I forgiven her just to get screwed over again? I will never know.

It has been three years since I've spoken to my mother. I wouldn't allow two days to go by with my own daughter without trying to make things right again. But not my mother. She has never apologized for anything, ever. I've never known any parent who bad-mouths their own children as much as mine does, and I hope another person like her doesn't exist. She also tried to make me feel inadequate as a mother and then told everyone who would listen that she was raising my daughter, which were complete and total lies that many people believed because she was a master at deception.

Mental note: Don't be this kind of a mom. If I only do one major thing in this world, Lord, please let this be it. Please, please let me be the one to break this cycle. Never let my daughter know what this feels like—not ever.

22

Luckily for me, there were good women in my life who were quite influential in shaping the better parts of me. The most influential woman for me was my Grandma Eva. She was the best grandma in the world. She accepted me and loved me for who I am. She made me feel like I was the one she loved the most, and I was the most important person in her world. I have a feeling she mastered making all her grandchildren feel this way. She even let me cook in her kitchen with her. I was only six when she died.

She taught this lefty how to crochet when I was only three years old. She let me sit on her lap facing her when she crocheted because I was so interested in watching her. My own mother never allowed me to sit on her lap, let alone put up with it when she was busy doing something. I still miss my grandma. I feel so robbed having her taken from me. Why is it the good ones go so soon?

My dad's Uncle Lawrence and Aunt Lillian lived in California in a small town called Hanford. We went to visit them every summer, and I loved spending time with Lillian. She was very much like my Grandma Eva. I think Lillian did her best to fill in the gaps where my grandma left off when she died. I have the best memories of her letting my brother and I take a handful of pennies out of her penny bowl. Then, one of the other cousins, either Mary Ann or Linda, took me down-town so I could spend them. I don't think they ever knew just how much this meant to me. It meant the world to me that they would take time out of their busy lives to spend time with me and make my short visit there so enjoyable. I learned from this experience that the best thing you can ever give a child is your time. It isn't expensive toys or electronics; it's just simply your time. The most valuable thing I have ever been given from special people in my life was their time. When I look back, these are the moments that mean the most.

Another woman I think of fondly is my Aunt Kathy. Uncle John and Aunt Kathy lived a couple of blocks from our house. She let me ride my bike over to her house so we could play Yahtzee while her baby was napping. I remember watching Aunt Kathy make her lunch and thought how lucky she was to get to have hamburgers for lunch. That was her cue to send me home for my own lunch. She probably needed a break from me anyway. I would have lived with them if I'd had a choice. It was actually a fantasy of mine as a kid. These women were iconic in helping to mold my life in a positive way. They showed me what good, loving mothers were all about. I think they had suspected things were bad at home but didn't have a clue just how bad it really was. I will always be grateful to these fine women for the time they gave me. They helped to mold the better parts of me.

Discord in the home is so damaging to a child. Coming from personal experience, it's so hard to have to listen to your parents yell at each other all the time. Children have an uncanny ability to make everything their fault. I used to think they were fighting over some-thing I must have done. I finally got to a point where I decided this was just their own unique way of communicating. This helped take the edge off blaming myself, but I still felt like I was living in a broken home. I can honestly say I would have rather come from a broken home than live in one. I wouldn't have even cared if the whole world knew it, too.

My father was so intensely secretive. My parents were all about keeping up pretenses. They always drove really nice cars, Mom was "dripping in diamonds," and she dressed in the finest clothes, as did both her children. My parents also lived by the motto, "Children should be seen and not heard." We were instructed whenever we went to anyone's home to never ask for anything to eat or drink, and if we needed to use the bathroom, we were told to come ask one of our parents.

Most of all, never, ever embarrass them or act out. Most of the time, we sat on the couch with our hands in our laps. We were scared to death we were going to screw up and then there would be hell to pay when we got home. I was terrified of them when they got angry. My father had this face that scrunched up, and he clenched his teeth together when he talked, but Mom was another story. Her eyes usually changed and got very dark. I used to say her eyes got black like her soul. To me, my mother is downright evil. That is the only way I can describe most of the things she has done to me. Maybe I shouldn't blame her at all. Maybe she has just been possessed by demons all these years. I'm not kidding. Her eyes turned black as night when she was angry. I have no explanation for it at all. Creepy is an understatement.

Outside appearances meant everything to my parents. I have heard my father say "This does not leave this house" more times than should be acceptable. In other words, don't you dare tell anybody what really happens here. I was usually so embarrassed by my mother's behavior that I rarely allowed any of my friends to come inside our house. I couldn't trust that she wasn't going to act crazy, and I couldn't risk losing another friend over it.

As a teen, she caused me to lose so many friends. She loved to call my friends and drill them about me. Many times, my friends just got to the point where they were sick of it, and the only way to really make it all stop was to stop being friends with me. Most of my friends were genuinely afraid of my mother. I feared her too, but most of the time I was just disgusted by her.

One of my mother's neighbors got to know me because our daughters were friends. One day, she saw me at the grocery store, walked over, and told me she wanted to confess something to me. She told me she had assumed I was just like my mother and admitted she used to hate me because of it. She said once she got to know me, she learned I was nothing like my mother and she felt bad for making the assumption. I guess it's guilt by association. I really respect her for making the confession. I don't think most people would admit that. I was used to apologizing to people for my mother's behavior—not that it was really my job, but I still felt guilty, embarrassed, and disgusted, therefore making it my responsibility.

Now that I am older, I think guilt is such a useless emotion. Seriously, how has it ever benefited anyone to feel this uncomfortable emotion? Guilt is pain and punishment all in one little word. Guilt is also the main thing I learned in Catholic school. Theresa told me that secrets are only meant to make people feel guilty. The more I think about it, the more I agree.

I wasn't necessarily as fearful of my mother as I got older, but the last thing I wanted was to be alone with her. When I was sixteen, we had to move to the Tri-City area in Washington state for my father's work. Dad had managed a local men's clothing store for longer than I'd been alive. He suspected the owner was thinking of selling the store, so Dad asked him if he would consider selling it to him. The owner said he would and promised to tell Dad when he was more serious about selling.

Well, that never happened, and the owner sold it out from under Dad's nose without giving him the chance to purchase it. What a cruel thing this was to do to my father. He had worked his butt off for this man for years. The store was sold to a partnership of three new owners that offered to let Dad stay on, but Dad knew eventually they just wouldn't need him anymore. He also felt like they just wanted him there for a short period of time to teach them how to manage the store. Dad put some feelers out there and found a new store to manage.

Unfortunately, it was in another state. I have never been faced with leaving my friends before. It was so difficult to leave them because they had really become family to me. My friends were my "love supply," and I didn't want to leave them. However, I also knew that Dad wouldn't have put us in this situation unless he had no other choice.

I always respected and loved my father a great deal and was grateful that at least I had one normal parent. Well, not completely perfect, but way more normal than Mom. Dad devoted his life to raising one family and then married Mom and worked his butt off to provide for ours. I really wish Dad could have had more of a backbone where Mom was concerned, though.

My father never had life turn out the way he wanted it to. He joined the Air Force at a young age because he wanted to someday go to school to fulfill his dream of becoming a dentist. They didn't have a lot of money, but there was a GI bill that helped with college. When dad was nineteen, he got a phone call from the red cross that informed him his father had died. Dad left the military with an honorable discharge and went home to help raise his two younger brothers. Dad was so selfless. He helped one brother go to Willamette Law School and the other brother was a successful JC Penney manager. Dad never fulfilled his own dream of becoming a dentist. Dad just sacrificed his own needs for everyone else.

Mom hated Washington even though Dad had purchased a brand new, beautiful home in a new development. She was rarely happy with anything. All of her expensive trinkets and diamonds only seemed to satisfy her for a short period of time.

One day, out of the blue, she decided to leave my father and move back to Oregon. My brother was working with Dad at the new store, so I was alone with Mom at home. After hearing her new plan, I was determined she was not going to take me with her. Even though going back would have meant going back to where my friends were, I simply could not bear the thought of having to be alone with my mother. I was in a very desperate situation and needed some help, desperately. I quietly went upstairs to my bedroom to secretly call Dad at work so I could tell him what was happening. Mom got up the stairs just in time to rip the phone cord out of the wall before I could give Dad the news. Not only did she rip the cord out of the wall, she also broke my phone. I had no way of calling anybody.

Now what am I going to do? How in the world am I going to get Dad home? I hate you so much, mom!

That was my very first little pink princess phone and my first time getting to have a phone in my own room. It was special to me and now it's broken. But, I am still in a desperate situation. How am I going to get Dad home to stop this and rescue me? I decided to fake an accident. I could pretend that I fell down the stairs and then she would have to call Dad and tell him to come home.

I stood at the top of the stairs practicing how I was going to fake my fall. I walked down to the middle of the stairs and was trying to figure out how to do it when my heel snagged a piece of carpet on the step and down I went. I landed with a boom on my behind on the slate entryway. So much for faking it.

I sat there thinking I had broken my butt. I yelled at Mom to call Dad at work to tell him it's an emergency and I need to go to the hospital. To my relief, she realized this was serious and made the call. Dad and my brother made it home pretty fast. I couldn't move off the floor. The pain was excruciating.

While I sat there in agony, my father walked into their bedroom and saw the suitcases on the bed that mom had placed there. Thank God! At least I was not in the car on my way back to Oregon with my mother. I honestly would much rather have a broken anything than to be alone in a car with her. I went to the hospital to find out I had, in fact, broken my tailbone. Luckily, the drama of my mother taking me and leaving was over.

I had to risk my butt to save my ass.

Dad realized something was terribly wrong and found a way to move us back to Oregon. We had only been in Washington for six months, but I had already made a lot of nice, new friends. Now I was sad to leave them. Dad found a better job as a regional manager of a men's clothing store back in Salem, and I took up right where I left off with all of my old friends back home. At sixteen, this was a lot of drama to go through. My old friends were so happy to see me that it made missing my new friends easier to take. At least we had moved back to the same area where my old high school was.

I tried out to be a cheerleader for the third time and finally made it. I really should have gotten an award for the amount of times I tried out for stuff. I tried out for nine plays and only made one. I had one line with four words in it. I was so proud of that one line. I tried out for drill team three times and never made it. It took me three times to make concert choir. I never gave up. I still don't. I am glad that I didn't give up, especially in high school, because I would have missed out on a lot of good times.

Even though Mom was happy to get to move back home, she revved up the crazy even more. She intensified her threats of suicide. I never truly understood why she liked to whisper the threats in my ear. Throughout my life, no matter how badly my brother and I begged Dad to get her the help she so desperately needed, he never did. I often wished I hadn't helped save their marriage back in Washington that day, but what was I supposed to do?

I was just a scared kid.

23

I am grateful for the person I am today, but I really did have to walk through a lot of shit to get here. I had been home for about a week after spending a month in the hospital with my first pancreatitis attack. I was still too sick to be going anywhere, that's for sure. I felt like I was near dying, and, when things got really bad in my life, I ran away. I ran away a lot as a kid. Sometimes, where I ran away to ended up being worse than what I was running away from.

I remember one time, late at night, I was so desperate to get away from my mother that I drove an entire hour to my brother's frat house. That was another night my mother attacked me. She scratched the backs of my hands so hard she made them bleed. I just felt I needed to talk to my big brother, someone who understood what Mom was like. My brother thought the best thing he could do to help me with my problems was to line me up some cocaine. I waited for him to line it up on a mirror. Then he handed me a rolled-up dollar bill and showed me how to snort it. I leaned over to snort it and blew the whole thing all over his room. I was so insulted. *How dare he do this to me. I am his little sister. He is supposed to protect me, not try to turn me onto drugs.* Luckily for me, I ran away from this too.

Anyway, I was really screwed up mentally, and I was trying to run away from myself, not my family, and I did everything wrong. I had started to develop a gambling problem before I got sick. Ever since the Indian casino was built, about a half hour away from where we lived, I was developing a problem. I was always intrigued by gambling because it was so much a part of my life growing up. Families back then used to take two-week vacations and we weren't any different. We would jump in the car and drive to California to visit family; however, on the way there, we always stopped in Reno.

Reno wasn't exactly "on the way," even though our parents tried to convince us it was. After our visit with family, we would go back to Reno for another couple of days. This isn't a fun place for kids. Our parents always plopped us right outside of the casino and made us wait there while they were inside playing the machines. Most of the time, we sat outside the Cal Neva casino in Reno. There were lots of other kids hanging out there too. It was the '60s, and no one was really concerned with our safety. My brother and I got pretty good at hustling the other kids with street craps. I was pretty good at craps and usually won, so it was a bit of a con. My brother would get bored and run into the casino to put a nickel in a machine, but a really big bouncer guy would always bring him back out. Those bouncers must have hated us kids sitting outside. We were such a pain in their butts, but it got really boring outside after a while, and really hot, too. I don't know if today that would be considered abuse or neglect or anything, really, but it was what we did every year. The casino became the forbidden fruit.

When I turned twenty-one, my father wanted to take me to Reno to teach me how to gamble. Dad and I stayed up all night putting quarters in a machine together. It may be the best memory I have of me and my father. For some reason, I loved to put money into a machine and watch the reels spin round and round. It was what I would consider an escape. I had spent a huge part of my life trying to escape. Now, all I have to do is put a little money into a machine and I escape. After the Indian casino was built, my parents invited me to go with them every Saturday, and most of the time I went.

By this time, Jeff and I were married and Stephanie was in middle school. I think Jeff didn't mind if I went as long as I didn't make him go, too. He never really cared much for gambling. He never played the machines, only blackjack. Blackjack bored me to tears, so I rarely played. I needed the excitement of the spinning reels. One time, I won about $2,500 on a machine. Later, I decided this was the worst thing that could have ever happened to me. All this did was encourage me to keep gambling. I loved the excitement, loved the possibility of another big win, but, most of all, I loved the escape. I needed the escape.

After a month in the hospital with a feeding tube and surgery to remove my gallbladder, I believed I could use a little escape. Plus, I had convinced myself I was going to die. I have pancreatitis and things weren't going well at all. I wasn't in excruciating pain anymore, but I still could barely eat without getting sick. I had absolutely no business going to Reno, especially not by myself. It's hard to explain what goes through a person's mind when they think they are close to dying.

Before my father died, he was told he had six months left. He asked me how I would feel if someone had told me that. I had no idea what to say. I wanted to find something soothing to say. Instead, what I said to him was something cheesy like, "As long as you are alive, there's hope." He died two months later in the hospital from emphysema. Right before he died, he kept kicking me out of his room because all he wanted to do was pray. I think he felt prayer would jet-propel him faster to heaven, but it actually broke my heart. I wanted time with him at the end. But I realized it wasn't about me. It was about him and what he needed to be comfortable. It really makes me sad that my last memory of my father was of him kicking me out of his room. He went into a coma later that day and we never talked again. I desperately needed a meaningful moment with him before he died.

I think I had a temporary loss of sanity. I went to the bank and took a seven-thousand-dollar draw on a credit card. This is a lot of money to us, and taking that amount off a credit card? Crazy. I didn't tell anyone until I got to Reno. I arrived around three in the morning and was exhausted. I got a cheap hotel room next to the Cal Neva, and, instead of sleeping, I went down to the casino. I barely slept the entire time I was there. I barely ate, too.

Every time I ate, I ended up in the bathroom sick for at least an hour. I called Jeff the next day to tell him where I was. I am still grateful for how kind he was to me. This was entirely selfish, and my own issues and fears led me there. I was trying to run away, but this time it was from myself. I remember thinking, *I will never come here again. This is the last time before I die.* I believed my pancreas was dying little by little, and the doctors always told me you can't live without your pancreas.

Stephanie was so angry with me for leaving that she went to talk to my parents. She needed some comforting and chose to look to them for it. She was gone a while and Jeff started to get concerned, so he drove over to check on her. My mother decided it was yet another great opportunity to bad-mouth and ridicule me. Sounds like she took full advantage of it. She said things to Jeff like, "You know she tried to kill herself, don't you?" and, "You knew she wasn't married when she got pregnant, didn't you?"

Luckily for me, I had already shared all the ghosts in my closet with Jeff. I am used to all this nasty stuff from my mother, but it was what my father said to Jeff that really hurt me. He told Jeff he should just have me committed—committed to a mental hospital. Maybe Dad was thinking more on the lines of an insane asylum from the 1950s. It was like my mother's words had come out of my father's mouth.

However, my father still needs to take responsibility for being the one to say it. I think, if Jeff were hearing this for the first time, it could have ruined us. This was her goal: she wanted to ruin us. Again, what kind of a mother does this stuff? Jeff told me later that she was so "into bashing me" that he really struggled to get her to stop. Even though Jeff had to have been extremely angry with me at the time, he still didn't appreciate her tearing me apart in front of my own daughter. That's a good man right there. He said it surprised him how "revved up" my mother got from the excitement of all my screwups. Jeff said he didn't care what I did before he knew me. I'm forever grateful to Jeff for how he handled things that day. *Thank you, Jeff, for having my back.*

I stayed in Reno for three days then decided to come home. I was getting sicker, and I hadn't slept much the entire time I was there. When I arrived home, Jeff was outside doing some yard work. He didn't have much to say to me and I don't blame him. I was too tired and sick to say much myself. Stephanie came home a few minutes later, and Jeff asked her if she had a couple of words for her mother.

"See ya later," she answered. Then she took off.

I feel horrible making my family feel this way. These were very dark times in all our lives, and I really hesitated sharing it with anyone. Maybe it's good to just get it out. Maybe someone else reading this is feeling the same way. I hope not, but if so, I hope my words can bring peace and hope for a better day. I think I just broke another cycle, the one my father held so dear when he said, "This does not leave this house." All I can say is, it's out of the house and gone for good.

Stephanie eventually came home, and boy did she have words for me then. I deserved every single one of them. I was lost and I needed to really listen to what my daughter was saying to me. She told me if Jeff and I got divorced, she was living with him. She told me that while I was away, Jeff started looking for an apartment for me to live in. She told me horrible, mean, angry things because I had hurt her and made her feel unsettled and unsafe. I decided to seek out a gamblers anonymous group and faithfully went to the meetings, stayed on track, and stopped gambling. I mended my relationship with my husband and daughter, and it has been wonderful ever since.

I am proud to say I overcame my gambling addiction. It's been over ten years. I believe people can recover and adapt to changing who they are as well as break cycles of abuse. However, I don't believe people can overcome all addictions then go back to them safely. But, some people can overcome theirs and handle it in small doses without becoming obsessed. I don't recommend this, however. It is rare, I think, but I have seen others do it. I am so grateful those days are way behind me now. It is still very painful to remember and talk about again. It's interesting how time really doesn't heal like I have always heard it does.

24

I wonder if any of my family will take the time to read my book. I am a very persistent person so I won't give up until I see my book in print. Maybe even the silver screen? Lights on Broadway? OK, it's fun to dream sometimes.

So, I never succeeded at becoming a doctor, but I am a damn good person who has suffered more than the average person and lived to tell about it. That should speak for something. I don't think it's fair to judge people solely on their profession. I judge them by how they act around me and how they treat me. Everyone should just remember there's only one Jesus, so let's get over the God complex. We are all the same here— nobody greater or lesser than anyone else. The worst feeling in the world is feeling like you don't deserve to be loved. Everyone has value and everyone deserves to be loved. For me, especially growing up, hearing negative talk over and over again made it my reality. Negativity is like gunk that jams up an engine. It creeps into your soul and somehow becomes who you are, but only if you allow it. Negative is stronger than positive for reasons I really don't understand.

Mother's Day has always been incredibly stressful. It always focused more on her than it ever did on me. I am a mother—my Mother's Day should matter, too—but not to my mother.

She could make life completely miserable. The day I didn't get to Mom's house until four in the afternoon because we decided to go to Jeff's mother's first really set her off. How dare we put his mother above her. Her reaction was to give my gift back to me. I had purchased her a flower planter with her name carved in wood. I told her I couldn't take it back because it had her name on it. Yes, it was always so embarrassing when she went on her rants in front of Jeff. He always tried to assure me it was fine, but I can only imagine what was going through his mind. Weird thing is, I never saw the planter again after that day. She must have trashed it.

Mom was an old pro at giving my gifts back to me. I remember that one year she gave me a ring back I had purchased for her at the State Fair. It was a turquoise ring, and I had spent all my fair money on it. I should have gone on the rides and enjoyed myself. Instead, I spent the entire time shopping for the perfect ring for her, and she just gives it back to me.

When I look back, it makes me so angry and sad all at the same time. I was so desperate for a mother to love me, and I was always trying to please her. I think I was trying to buy her affection like I always saw my father do. But it was a cheap State Fair ring, the kind you could adjust the size by squeezing it and then eventually it turns your finger green. I pleaded with her to keep it. I was only nine years old and didn't really understand why she didn't want it.

Years later, I realized she didn't want it because it wasn't a nice, expensive "jewelry store" ring and wasn't good enough for her. Broke my heart so much. She should have worn that ring with pride. How many kids spend their entire fair money on their mom? Probably only desperate children like me.

Another time I made her a bouquet of bachelor button flowers I'd picked from the side of a steep hill. This was a really steep hill, and I almost fell down it trying to pick them, but these were really pretty, blue flowers, so I risked it. When I gave them to her, she informed me that these weren't really flowers, they were just weeds, and she threw them away.

I can't imagine doing that to my daughter. I would have worn that ring with pride and felt so honored that my child spent her fair money on her mom instead of all the fun things she could have done. So what if the pretty blue flowers were just weeds? I didn't know they were weeds, and I didn't need the education at the time. I needed my mom to appreciate my efforts and love me for it. I never knew unconditional love growing up. Even up until the time I cut her out of my life, it was based on a "what have you done for me lately" attitude. I am so grateful that I didn't carry this attitude on with my own daughter. I couldn't even if I tried because I love her so much.

My husband, Jeff, is hugely responsible for helping me regain some self-esteem. He says, "Don't believe your parents' press clippings," or, "You're not the horrible person they make you out to be." He also says, "Don't let miserable people get you down."

Depending on which time in our lives you choose, my brother and I have taken turns being the worst people in the history of the world, according to my mother. My father never stepped in to save us because that would have turned her vengeance on him, and he couldn't allow that to happen. He allowed us kids to take it instead. He basically sacrificed his own children so he didn't have to take the wrath.

This stuff got into my head and messed me up for a very long time. I wonder if it's because when you are a young child, you believe what your parents say about you, and, even though it's negative, it still must be true. It's not until you get older that you realize your parents are just human and have flaws too, but by then the negative message is ingrained into who you are. This can be changed, however, even to my amazement, and I owe a great deal of it to my husband Jeff.

25

After I got away from my abusive ex-husband, I decided to get some counseling. I was terrified that I was somehow subconsciously attracted to abusive men. I wasn't sure if I ever wanted another relationship, but if it did happen, I wanted to protect myself and my sweet girl from any more abuse. I went to counseling for two years, and I am glad I did. I just focused on improving myself and didn't date anyone the entire time. I was very content being a mom, although it did get a bit lonely at times, especially on the weekends when Stephanie was away. However, I would rather be alone and lonely than in another abusive relationship.

During this time, I decided to seek counseling. I strongly believe in counseling, especially when you find someone you feel comfortable with. This wasn't exactly easy for me. Remember: I wasn't supposed to tell any family secrets. Hide it, hold it all inside, and don't show any weakness. I also had too much experience with a mother who gladly gossiped everything I recklessly shared with her. You can imagine how tough it was at first to feel comfortable trusting someone. Requirements were that the counselor had to be a woman. I couldn't talk to any man about my rape, or anything else for that matter. The person I found was a kind, nonjudgmental woman, and she treated me with respect. Life gives you lemons sometimes. Don't make lemonade; just go get some professional help.

You can meet your soul mate in the strangest places and when you least expect it. I was just going through life, busy with work, raising my daughter, and making ends meet. The last thing on my mind was finding a man. I was working full-time at a local mortgage loan office as the assistant to the president. The salary wasn't very much despite what it sounds like, so I had to find other ways to make ends meet. The child support order remained only $103 a month, and it was a year behind.

I hated ever having to ask my parents for money. My mother used to love making me feel like a piece of shit if I ever asked. I would almost rather beg on the street before I would ever want to ask her for anything. On top of making me feel like the biggest loser on the planet, my mom constantly reminded me that I was in her debt. She acted like I owed her something, which was usually my soul or peace of mind. Believe me, she took full advantage of it. She would come up with "favors" she knew I wouldn't want to do, but then throw it in my face that she had just loaned me money. She always kept score. She also liked to make me feel like I wasn't capable of being a mother solely because I was poor and often threatened me with taking my child away.

I tried to come up with other creative ways to earn money. I love crafts and crocheting, so I started crocheting angels. They were gorgeous tabletop angels that were then starched to stand up. I made these angels all year, then sold them at various holiday craft shows before Christmas. I made decent money doing this, but it was only seasonal.

Another job I had was selling jewelry in home jewelry shows. I didn't hate doing this, but it was a lot of work, and selling to women can be challenging. Pleasing women, I found, is not an easy job. They can be very critical. But, I needed the money so I kept going. I did really well and even inspired a couple of other women to work under me as sales agents. This was a pyramid scheme, of course. The more people I brought on to work under me, the more commission I would earn. This part didn't really appeal to me as much. I just focused on getting those shows booked and, if the women were interested, I would certainly help them with their businesses as well.

I will never forget this one particular jewelry show. I always started with a presentation showing different pieces of jewelry. Out of the blue, this woman totally interrupts me to run out to her car to get a shirt. I tried to keep going on with my presentation, but the other women in the room decided to get up and move around too. I have never had a show go quite like that one. The customer who ran out to her car drove me crazy. She was loud, disruptive, and had a million questions. She wanted a necklace to match the shirt she had just purchased. A couple weeks later, she called me to say she hated the necklace. I offered to let her have the one I had on display at the show. She was content with that, so I drove it over to her house.

When I knocked on the door, I was greeted by a man. I asked if my customer were there.

"She's in the kitchen," he answered and walked away. The screen door was still closed. He didn't even open it for me.

I thought, *How rude!* I walked through the door and into the kitchen. My customer was busy making Christmas candy with a friend. I traded the necklace with her and she was finally happy with it. I didn't notice any difference between the necklace she ordered and the one I gave her, but as long as my customer was happy, I was too.

I noticed that the guy who answered the door was sitting in a room off the kitchen alone with a beautiful yellow lab. I was immediately drawn to the dog, so I walked in to pet the dog. We began to chat and he introduced himself. His name was Jeff.

After I left, I began to think differently about Jeff. He wasn't so bad after talking to him. He was very cute, too. There was a real sadness about him that bothered me. I wondered if he was so rude to me at the door because he was sad and lonely. I assumed he was married to my customer, so I went home and tried to get him off my mind. I just couldn't stop thinking about him, though. The next day, I got a call from my customer. She told me they were married but in the process of getting a divorce.

"Would you be interested in going on a date with Jeff?" *She actually asked me this.*

I said, "This is weird," but inside I was excited because I liked him. So, I answered, "Tell him to give me a call."

Sure enough, he called me within a half hour and we made a date. Jeff took me on what I refer to as my best date ever, and he's the last person I ever dated. I think I fell in love with him on our first date. First of all, he took me to my favorite restaurant, which blew me away. He didn't know a thing about me, so I was immediately impressed. We had a great dinner with absolutely zero awkward silence the entire time. We went to see a movie afterward, and he was a total gentleman. He didn't try to kiss me, or hold my hand, and I appreciated the respect he showed me. Our shoulders barely touched during the movie, and I will always remember that because I thought it was so romantic. He even opened the door for me and treated me like a lady.

I truly believe it was working on myself and staying away from men for two years that helped me move past self-destructiveness. Jeff was a really good guy, but before I got help, I probably wouldn't have given him a chance.

Jeff and I started dating, but he was just getting over a marriage so he wanted to take things slow. That was OK with me. I had a daughter to think about. We didn't go out on a lot of dates. Instead, we talked on the phone every night. We got to know each other really well by just talking on the phone. We talked while he did his laundry, ironed his shirts, and made his dinner. It used to make me gag a little the meals he made for himself. He fried up hash browns, then broke eggs over them and fried them all together. *Disgusting*, I would think. The best part of our relationship is how much we have always laughed together. He became my best friend over the phone.

Jeff said he fell in love with me the night I fed him some cold, left-over grilled chicken when he had a fever of almost 103 degrees. He was so sick and weak, the coldness of the food felt good with his fever, and he loved being taken care of. We had probably only dated about six months by this time. I think he fell in love with me a lot sooner, but he was just too gun-shy to admit it. I told him he fell in love with me because I bought him a set of Ping golf clubs for Christmas with my craft show money. It was like we already knew each other, like we were

THIS DOES NOT LEAVE THIS HOUSE

old souls coming together again after a long time apart. There wasn't even the tiniest moment of awkward silence.

We had been dating for two years. I wasn't getting any younger or any more beautiful, so I told him to "shit or get off the pot." Classy, I know, but come on: either marry me or move on. I really wanted a family for myself and Stephanie, who was almost eight years old. Some guys just need a little nudge. Later, he told me he went for a long drive out in the country to think about it. I knew he would be a great father to Stephanie, which he is.

One Sunday afternoon, we were sitting in front of the TV watching football.

"So," Jeff turned to me casually. "You think we should get married?"

I smiled and answered, "Yes!" Then I broke out in tears.

I let Jeff plan the wedding. I didn't really care about the ceremony. We had both been married before, and I just wanted to get on with our lives together. Jeff found a pastor to marry us in the yellow pages. It cost us twenty-five dollars total. We could only have six guests at the wedding and no rice was allowed. The church was behind a tire store. This sounded so hick to me. When I walked into the church, I had to laugh because the carpet was blue-and-green shag. The pastor drove up in a little white clown car that had a magnetic sign on the side that read *Wedding Chapel*. I didn't even buy a wedding dress. I just picked a dress out of my closet that I already had. Jeff especially loves to answer the question, "How did you meet?" with "My wife introduced us." I don't remember the ceremony that much, but the part after I will always remember.

We opened our two wedding presents in the parking lot, then drove to the beach in Lincoln City for our one-night honeymoon. I had honeymooned at the same beach when I married my first husband. *Let's hope this honeymoon turns out a little nicer.* We stayed at a hotel that had a nice restaurant and a band was performing in the bar the same night. We got married on a Sunday. We arrived at our hotel around four in the afternoon. I was ready for a nap, and Jeff wanted to go explore a nearby golf course. While he was out, I took a nap. By the time he returned, I was starving and ready for dinner. Jeff and I had planned to eat dinner at the fancy steak restaurant at the hotel. Jeff got hungry while he was out looking at the golf course and decided to go to a McDonald's drive-thru. Even though he'd just eaten a McDonald's value meal, he didn't make me wait for our fancy dinner. He ate two dinners that night.

After dinner, we drove around the tiny beach town of Lincoln City looking for something to do. Nothing was going on in that tiny beach town on a Sunday night. The only thing to do was to go back to the bar at our hotel and watch the band. When I told our server that we had just gotten married that day, she immediately went and told the band leader, who announced it to the entire bar. It was so sweet. Everyone was so happy for us, and the drinks started filling up our table. The drinks were very impressive, too. I had never seen a flaming drink before that night. So many drinks were sent to our table—so, so many.

I don't remember much, other than waking up hugging the toilet. Jeff woke up starving. I couldn't imagine eating anything yet. I was so hungover. However, I owed it to him since he went to dinner for me last night. We drove to a little greasy spoon restaurant, and the second I walked in the door I felt sick. I didn't want our first day as a married couple to be a total disaster, so I powered on. I sat there and ordered breakfast. I thought maybe a little grease would do me good. "Grease is a great thing for a hangover," Jeff tells me. He said he always felt better after eating a hamburger from a fast food restaurant when he was hungover. So, I kept trying to handle it, but when the food arrived, I just had to get out of there. I couldn't stand to even look at it, let alone smell it.

I went and sat in the car, which just happened to be parked right across from our table. I sat there and watched Jeff eat his breakfast— and mine too. We drove to the Oregon aquarium and walked around for a while. I began to feel a little better. Then, all of a sudden, I was famished. I felt like I hadn't eaten in days. I felt a ton better after I ate, and I was happy that the day wasn't a complete disaster.

❧ 26 ❧

It isn't the big, expensive wedding that makes the marriage; it's the people in it. I love our wedding story because it's kind of silly and goofy like we are, even though it was probably the cheapest wedding in the history of the world. I call Jeff my "reward from God." My family refers to him as "Saint Jeff" because he married me. He really is my blessing and the best thing that has ever happened to me, aside from Stephanie. I have a little family now based on unconditional love and total support. We don't judge each other; we just love each other. This was a dream come true for me. Jeff and Stephanie bonded over sports. Jeff helped coach her girls softball team, and Jeff and I helped keep score at her volleyball tournaments. Jeff went to every game. I missed a few due to my illness, but not many.

I loved watching her play. She is such a natural athlete, and I was always so proud to be her mom. I have zero athletic ability, so I am in awe of her. I was always the kid picked dead last during P. E. class. I get it: I wouldn't want me on the team either.

Stephanie was a very good pitcher. She played mostly first base or pitcher on her softball team. She took pitching lessons, and when Jeff couldn't take her, I did. One day at her lesson, her teacher told all the other girls to stop and watch me. I often was comic relief for the pitching class. First of all, I'm sitting on this bucket watching a ball coming at my head at what seemed like a zillion miles per second. That almost knocked me off the bucket a few times. The teacher thought it was so funny that I would catch the ball (if I could catch it, that is), and then have to stop, remove my mitt, and then throw the ball back, and, yes, I throw like a girl. I am a lefty who pitches and catches with my left hand. Poor Stephanie. I'm sure she hated it when her mom had to be the one to take her to her lessons.

I loved being at her games, even in the rain. I have no memory of my mother ever coming to see me when I was a cheerleader in high school. I remember my father being there a couple of times in the stands, but never her. I always looked to see if either one of my parents showed up.

Speaking of sports, I know basically nothing about sports, so it made for some interesting moments when I was a cheerleader. I was cheering one night at a basketball game, and one of the cheers I decided to start was, "First and ten, do it again." Embarrassing myself came quite naturally and regularly. It was OK with me as long as they weren't being mean when they laughed at me.

I loved it when I could make people laugh and I still do. I decided to be on the powderpuff football team when I was a senior in high school. Again, not knowing anything about football, it was just something I wanted to do with my friends. I practiced and practiced being the hiker. The boys on the varsity football team were teaching us senior girls how to play. It was going to be the seniors against the juniors. One day, one of the boys came up to me and told me they had decided on what position I would be playing. I said, "Am I gonna get to be the hiker?" He finally said, "We picked your position. You're going to play center." I was so disappointed. *What is this "center?" I wanted to be the hiker. All my practice down the drain.* He couldn't stop laughing to get the words out, but finally he said, "Julie, center is the hiker, you dope."

My father was so excited to come watch me. He actually took time off work in the middle of the afternoon, and he had never done that before. The day of the game comes and I see my father sitting in the stands. I wave at him, bend down to hike the ball for the first play of the game and then . . . *rip*. When I bent over, my pants ripped out down the entire back seam. I had to run off the field, into the girls dressing room, and sit there until the game was over. My father had taken the day off to come see me bend over, rip out my pants, and end my football career. *Sorry, Dad. Not exactly how I intended to impress you today.*

I know it sounds like my childhood was all dread and sadness. There were many dark days, it's true, and most days were filled with drama and anxiety. However, I do need to acknowledge some good days as well. Even if the good was just for a little while, it's still important because the negative can easily overpower the positive. It was really hard growing up with a mother like mine, but let me take a moment to try to come up with something positive.

I remember a trip to Disneyland that was fun. I don't remember too much drama on this trip either. My father was pretty funny one day when we went to a drive-thru restaurant off the freeway to get some cold drinks. I wanted a grape slush and he ordered a grape flush. Well, maybe mentally he was already in Reno. No matter where our destination was for the two-week family summer vacation, Reno was always the first and the last stop along the way.

I loved Disneyland so much I wanted to live there. My father had to carry me out of there at the end of the day. I have great memories of visiting family in California and the women along the way who tried to make up for the mother I had. Nobody ever talked about it, but I am sure everyone knew something was off with my mother.

What I am trying to say is this: in the middle of the darkness, always try to find the lighter side of things and try to be a positive force for yourself. Unfortunately, I was a kid and had no resources to help save me. I ran away a few times but never for long. Luckily, I probably had some divine spirits looking after me as a young child, and they protected me from the dangers of being a runaway.

There were other things that I did to get through it. I loved to read books, and I could easily lose myself in my books. I also loved to play the piano because of my Grandma Eva. She really influenced the better parts of me. I used to pound on the piano at her house before she died, and she would make up songs to go along with my noise. I started piano lessons when I was nine and took nine years of lessons. I could really escape through my music. It was a great gift to have and something I could be proud of. I was scared to death to perform, but piano was something I could go escape into for a little while. I would close myself off inside a tiny room and just relax and play my piano. I don't play anymore, and some days I really regret that. I had a piano, but I pretty much sold everything of any value when Stephanie was little because we were so poor and needed the money.

Even though I consider myself a "recovering Catholic," I still have a strong faith in God and consider myself very spiritual. However, I still feel very angry at the things that I, along with the other kids in Catholic school, had to endure.

I was diagnosed with PTSD recently. I try not to let it control my life or even give it any power over my life. Along with the panic attacks, that's a lot to deal with. Believing in yourself and fighting against it is so important. Getting help is also important. When I took a job at a bank, I woke up with panic attacks the first two weeks after starting. I called for counseling every morning to help get me through. Panic attacks are horrible. The worst part is, I convince myself that I am dying every time. It's horrifying, to put it mildly.

Why is it that people who do the most horrible things to other people, especially when it pertains to children, have others who are willing to keep their secret hidden? I'm referring to the Catholic Church and the child molestation scandal. Also, when my cousin tried to rape me, why did my family choose to sweep it under the carpet and not help me bring him to justice? They never even talked to me about it. My father just wanted it to all go away. Heck, I would have loved for it to all go away and finally give me some peace. However, time heals nothing, and their silence never helped me either.

You can't change the spots on a leopard. The leopard has spots so it can hide. There is no closure without peace and no peace without justice. Nothing is more frustrating than to feel like you have no closure, no justice. I have decided to leave it all in the hands of divine justice. I am happy to say I still have a lot of love in my heart, which is odd to me after all the experiences I've had and how much pain I've suffered. I think I have yearned for love most of my life. I also learned you need to give it to receive it. The good, and even the bad, experiences in my life were lessons to get me to who I am today. Everything happens in life for a reason. Hard to understand, but I believe there are no coincidences. I hope my experiences help champion you in your own journey through this life.

Unfortunately, I come from very physical, emotional, and mentally abusive relationships. However, I miraculously never allowed it to mold who I am. I never used the excuse that I was abused as a kid to give me the green light to be an abuser as an adult. Don't limit yourself by excusing your behavior or by copping out. I was afraid if I ever spanked my daughter, I would never stop, and that terrified me pretty much out of ever disciplining her. I'm sure I didn't discipline her enough, but I would rather be that way than abusive. Instead, I have broken more than one cycle of abuse and for that I am thankful, a bit surprised, and very proud. I love the thought that this will benefit generations long after I am gone. For me, it feels like a very remarkable thing to accomplish. My self-esteem never allowed me to think I would amount to much, let alone fix something this important. I want to change the theme of people being abused then growing up to be the abusers. It doesn't have to be this way.

People can and do change. I am not exactly sure yet how to go about doing this, but I want to change the world and make abuse a thing of the past for everyone. I hope beyond hope that I can help people through relating my story. I want to enable them to put together a plan to end abuse forever in their lives and many lives after them. Stand up and fight against abuse and get it out of your life. Speak your truth, reject this in your life, and rise up. No matter how hard this sounds, it can be done. If I can do it, anyone can do it. Rise up against abuse. Give yourself the power and take control of your life back. Don't stand for another day of misery. Please, take my story and heal from it.

Anything is possible . . .

"What peace there may be in silence." I love the poem, *Desiderata*. I read it often. It is a very wise, old poem. Desiderata was written in 1927 by Max Ehrmann. The word *desiderata* means "things that are desired." I love the ending: "With all its sham, drudgery and broken dreams it is still a beautiful world. Be cheerful. Strive to be happy."

This one little sentence says so much: "What peace there may be in silence." I wish my parents had read that sentence when I was a kid. I really could have used a little silence back then. I got so tired of hearing them yell at each other all the time.

If you are in a bad marriage full of yelling and abuse, get out. Don't con yourself into thinking you should stay for the children. It's quite the opposite. A child would rather be from a broken home then live in one. I heard Doctor Phil say that one day on his show and I agree. It was like someone was finally speaking out for me. Children are aware there are problems no matter how much parents believe otherwise. They know everything that's going on.

If you are a parent now, live your life for the betterment of your kids. You have been blessed with a very important gift, so treat it with love and special care. Treat them as you would want to be treated. Don't ever forget the magnitude of your responsibility not to mess up their little lives. If you are doing the fighting, your children are paying the price for it.

Believe me, time will not heal their wounds.

❦ 27 ❦

I don't really have a lot of words of wisdom. All I have is my personal story. Hopefully, my experience can save someone else and give hope that things can and do change for the better. I have heard the only constant in life is change. If I am able to help even one other person, it makes all the hell I have been through in my life worth it. I am willing to walk through fire to help another person. Every time something bad happens to me, I'm convinced I am the only one on the planet experiencing it, but, unfortunately, that's not true at all. Too many people in this world are suffering, and life is just too darn short to put up with it. Let the secrets out, change the cycle, and you will make life more pleasant for yourself and especially for your children.

When I look back on my life, there sure has been a lot of drama. I'm grateful that I finally get to have so much hope and promise for the second half of my life. I enjoy life so much more today since I got away from the abusers and negative influencers in my life. I have a very loving little family now, and I am so happy being a grandma, too. There was so much stress when Stephanie was little just trying to make ends meet as a single mother.

I have also noticed that Stephanie is a much more relaxed mother than I was. I see so much of my daughter in Eva, too. It's interesting how being a grandma feels like reliving your own child's childhood and seeing how much they are alike. Eva will be the second generation to benefit from the cycles I was able to break, and that warms my heart beyond words. It's like a gift you can leave your family forever. What could possibly be better than that?

When I think that I accomplished being the hero in my family, I feel so proud. I changed not one but two cycles of abuse, and that rarely happens, if ever. I absolutely cannot think of a better gift. I want everyone who experienced abuse as a child to grow up with the intent to break the cycle for the next generations to come. There really isn't a more amazing and wonderful feeling than this.

My motivation came out of fear, but at least it still changed the future. When Stephanie thanked me for breaking the cycle, it made me feel so amazingly good. I will never forget it. The self-confidence that comes with improved self-esteem is way overdue. I am still a work in progress, and I know there is a long way to go, but this is a great start.

Every time you can do something to make you feel proud of yourself, you help chip away some of the negative stuff that has attached so deeply to your soul. Keep chipping away and stop allowing miserable people to get you down. It's time for a change. "And no message could have been any clearer, if you wanna make the world a better place, take a look at yourself, and then make a change." Thank you, Michael, for these great words of wisdom.

I would like to share some of my personal thoughts and ideas for how to get started, to stop the cycle of abuse. It's one thing to say just stop the cycle, but how do you get started? Where do you possibly begin?

The golden rule of "do unto others as you would have them do unto you" is one of the most powerful rules to follow. Empower yourself. It might be the very first time in your life, so pledge to take your power back. Don't make this too big of a chore. Enjoy doing this for yourself. Think of this as a gift you not only give yourself but also to the people you love in your family. Don't make excuses. It's a choice to be a certain way. Don't limit yourself. Stop accepting the old tape of "It's all

I know" or "I was abused so it's natural that I'm an abuser." Make a conscious effort and pledge to change life for the better for your children.

Write down a list of all the things that were done to you when you were a child that you hated, then vow to never repeat those behaviors. Make this promise every day. Eventually, positive actions will start replacing the negative ones until they become a new normal. This could impact many generations to come, and it started with you. My parents' attitude toward raising kids is that they "own" the children and have total control over them. I owed them for giving me life. However silly that sounds, they believed it. There have been times in my life where I've noticed one single person has made a huge impact in the world. Whether it be good or bad, it can be done.

Make a decision to lead in the movement to stop cycles of abuse. People are also afraid of change. Even if it's for the better, people are still more comfortable with what they know. Abuse loves this because it keeps it perpetuating throughout the generations. Wouldn't it feel amazing to know that you were responsible for ending something so horrible? Wouldn't you love to make life more enjoyable and peaceful for your family of the future? But many don't. It is all they know. Well, it's time someone made a stand and stood up against this.

You can't control how others behave, but you can control how you react to it. Look at your own wounds and begin to heal them, one wound at a time. Release the pain and make it a rebirth for yourself so your family can reap the rewards. Take responsibility for yourself and work toward being someone you can look up to and be proud of.

Be the hero for your family.

The journey starts with you. This can be scary and not always pleasant, but it needs to be done. Who better to do it than you? You know what it's like to be abused and you know exactly how you deserve and want to be treated. Don't waste another day being miserable. As you grow and see yourself more clearly, you realize it's you that has raised the bar to behave in a manner of respectability. This is where you can begin to change those around you, and hopefully, society as a whole. Lead by example and you can affect the destiny of the world.

Stop hiding the "family secrets." Get them out there and parade them around so everyone can see how ugly they really are. You can't change anything if you don't acknowledge it. One person really can make a difference. I want to be that one person and create a domino effect, so everyone will join in. I hope we can all join together to start a movement of positive change in the world. Let's work together to plant the seed and watch it grow. Life is a beautiful thing when there isn't any abuse in it. Stop making excuses for the abuser. Stop continuing to enable them. Get it out there and get on with it.

Don't you cry no more.

ABOUT THE AUTHOR

Julie Coons is a wife, mother, and grandmother who lives in a small town in Oregon. She hopes to eventually travel the world while spreading the important message of ending the cycle of abuse.

If you wish to connect, ask a question, or invite Julie to speak to your group or organization, contact her at connect@juliecoons.com or visit juliecoons.com.

NEXT STEPS

I'm a new author, and I hear reviews are like gold to writers. Would you please help me and leave me a review? Thank you!

Made in the USA
Middletown, DE
15 June 2020

97822567R00106